wildart coloring book

BY COLOURED WITCH

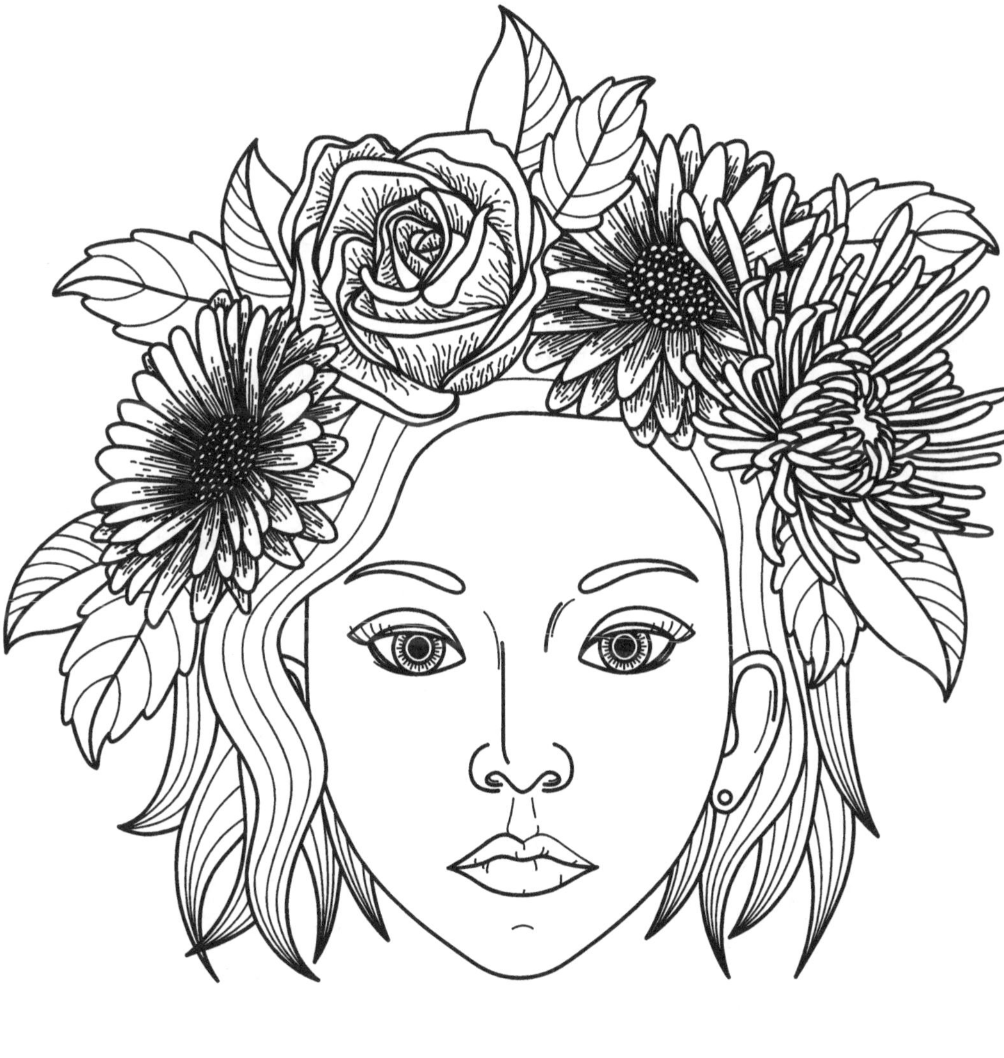

YOUNG HEART ARTS

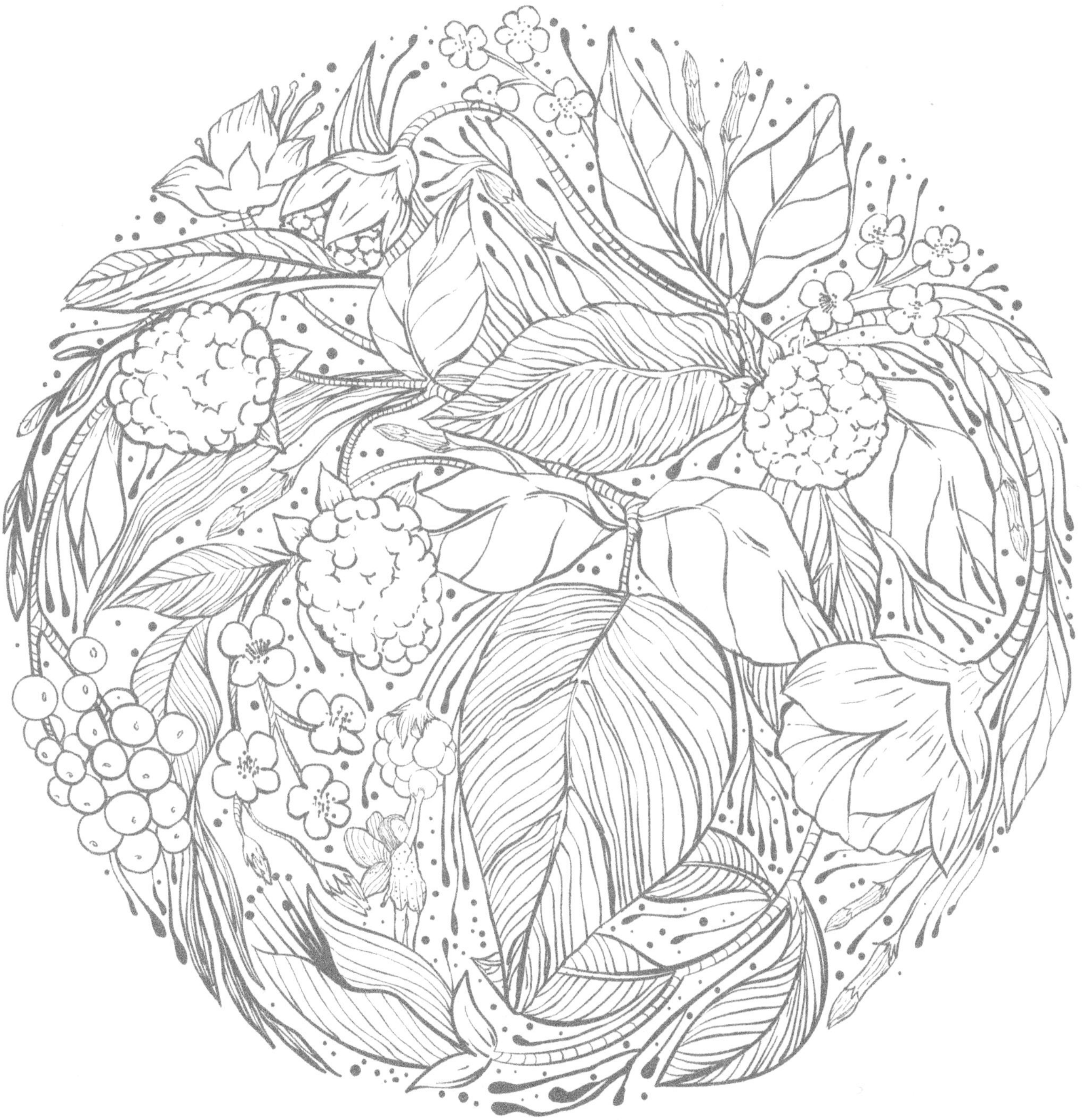

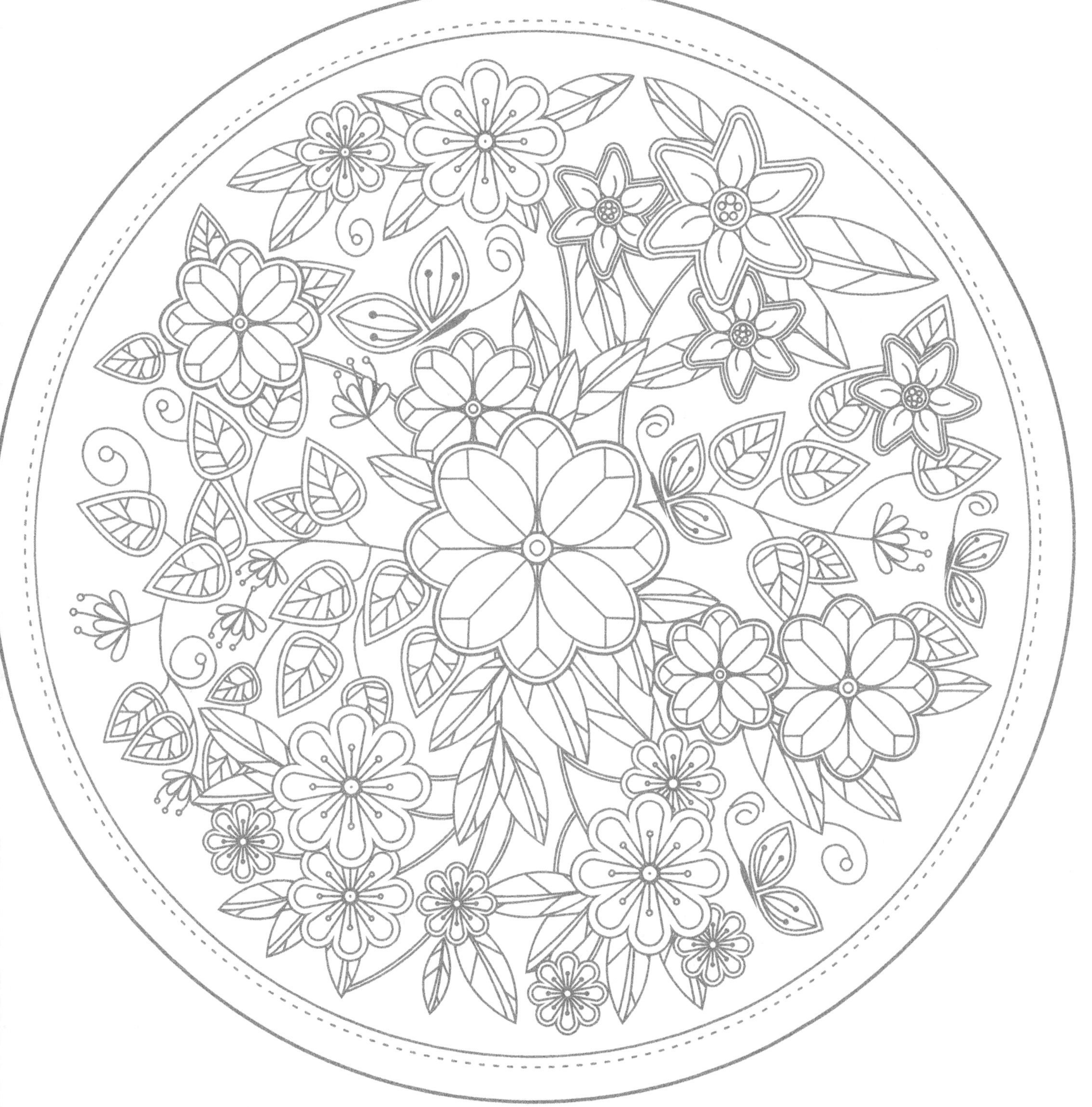

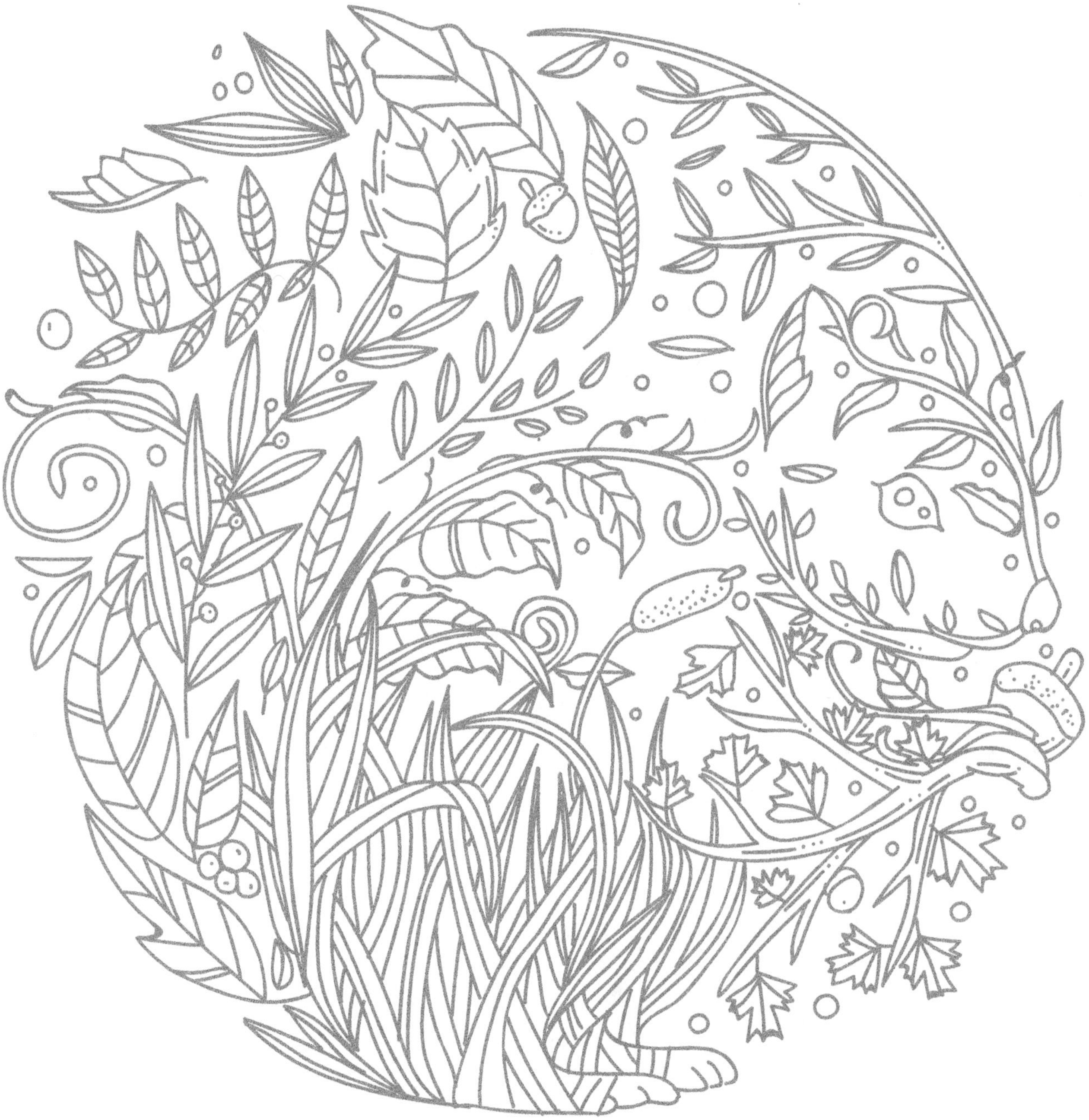

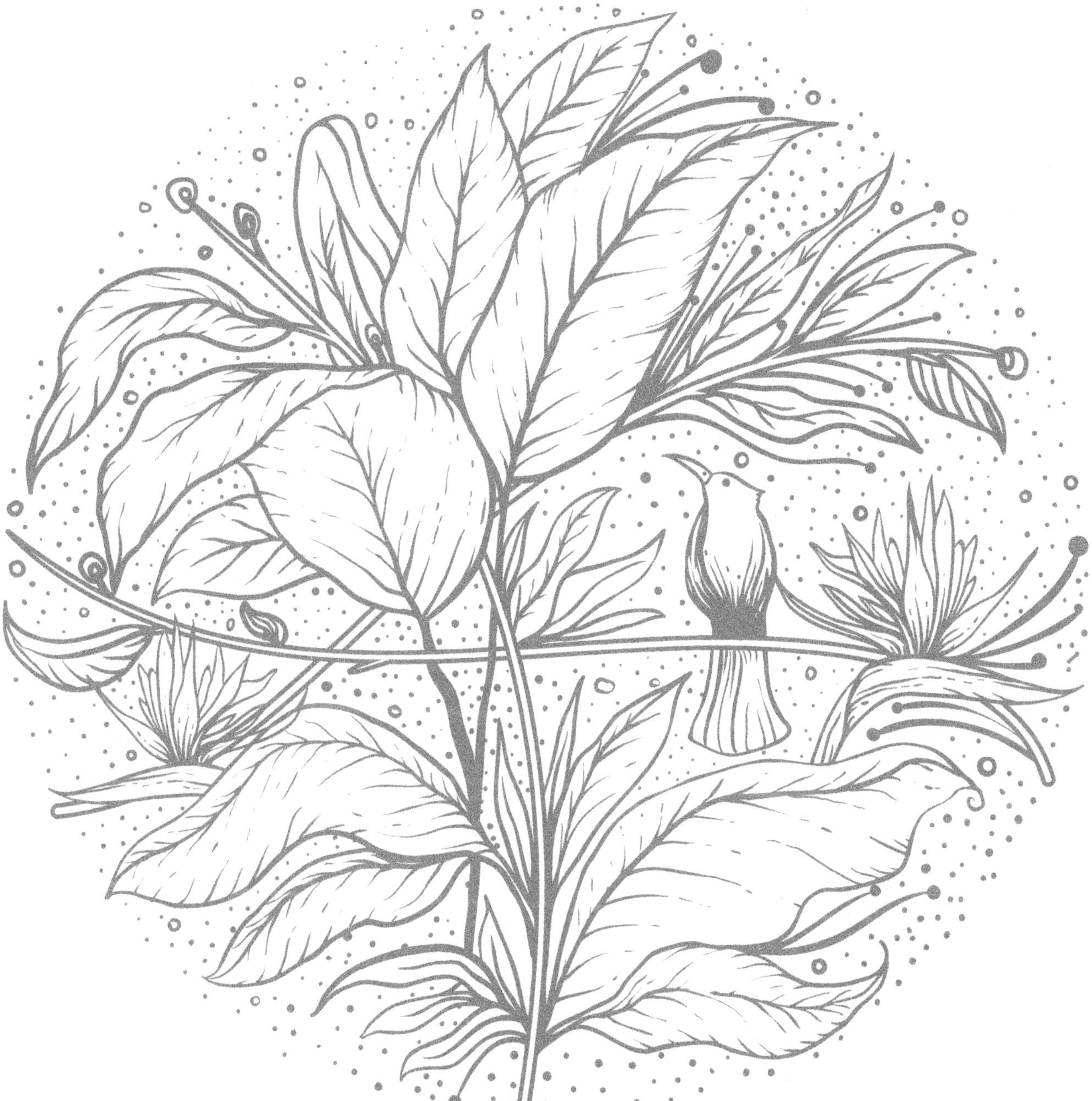

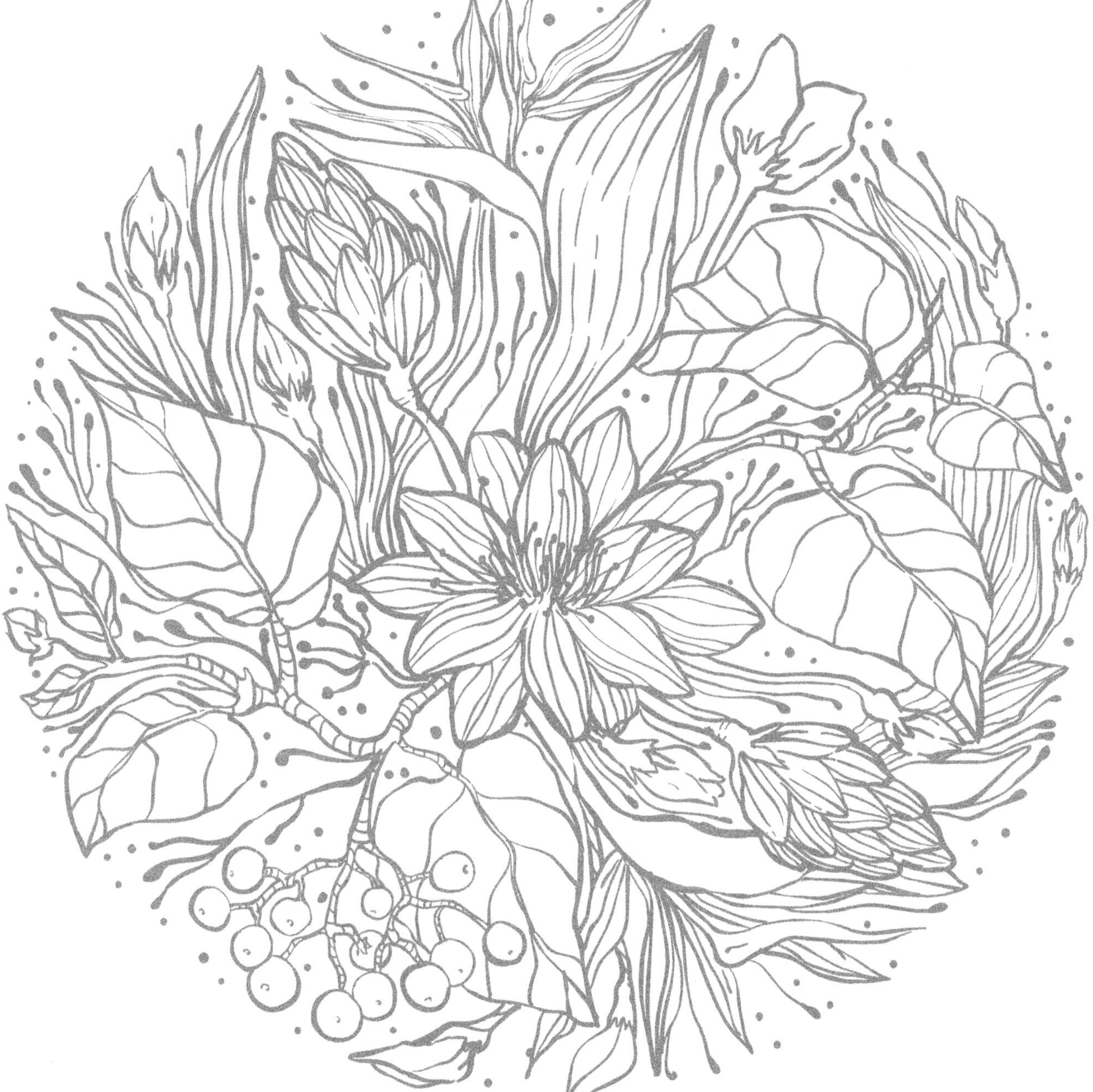

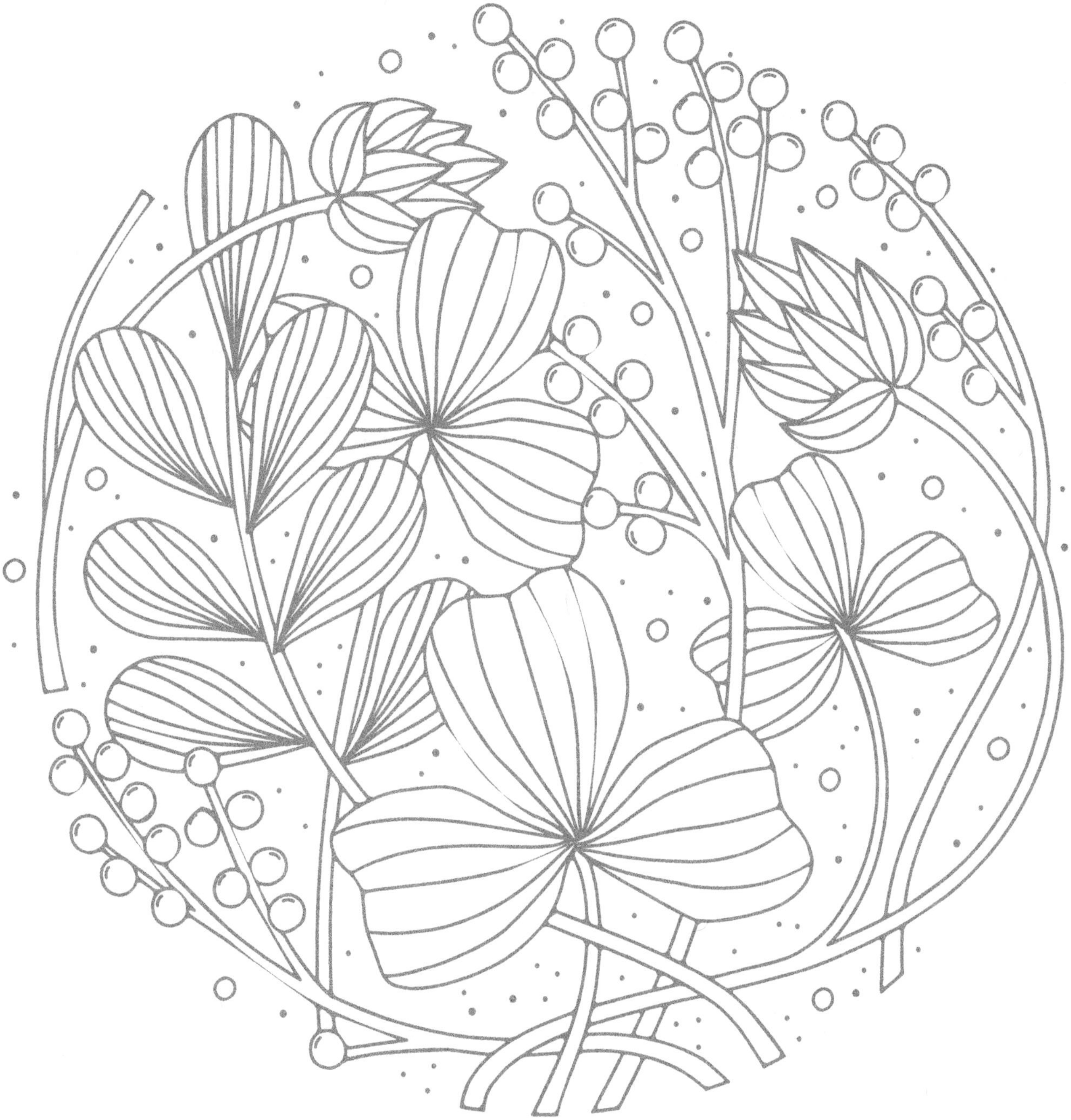

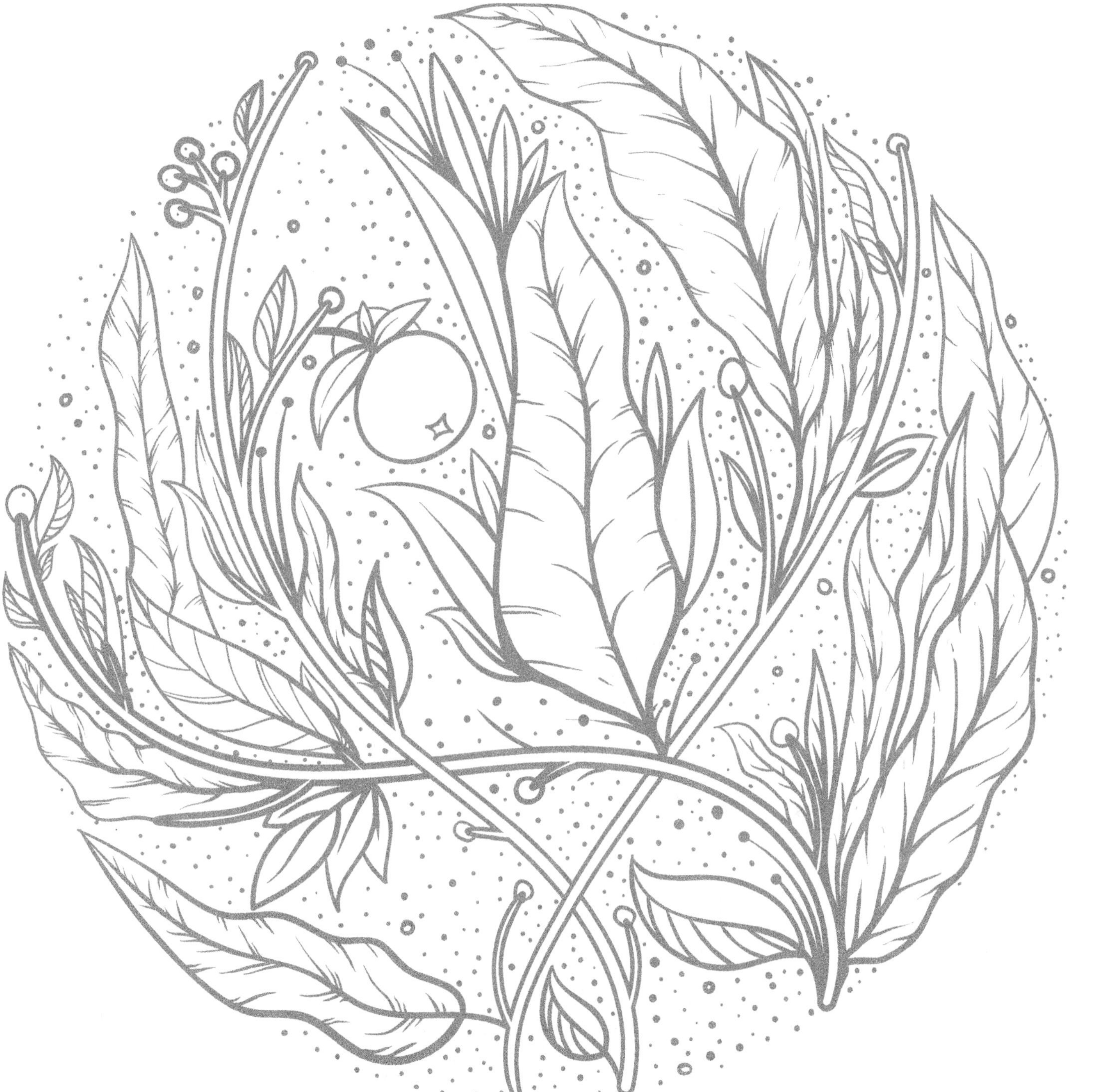

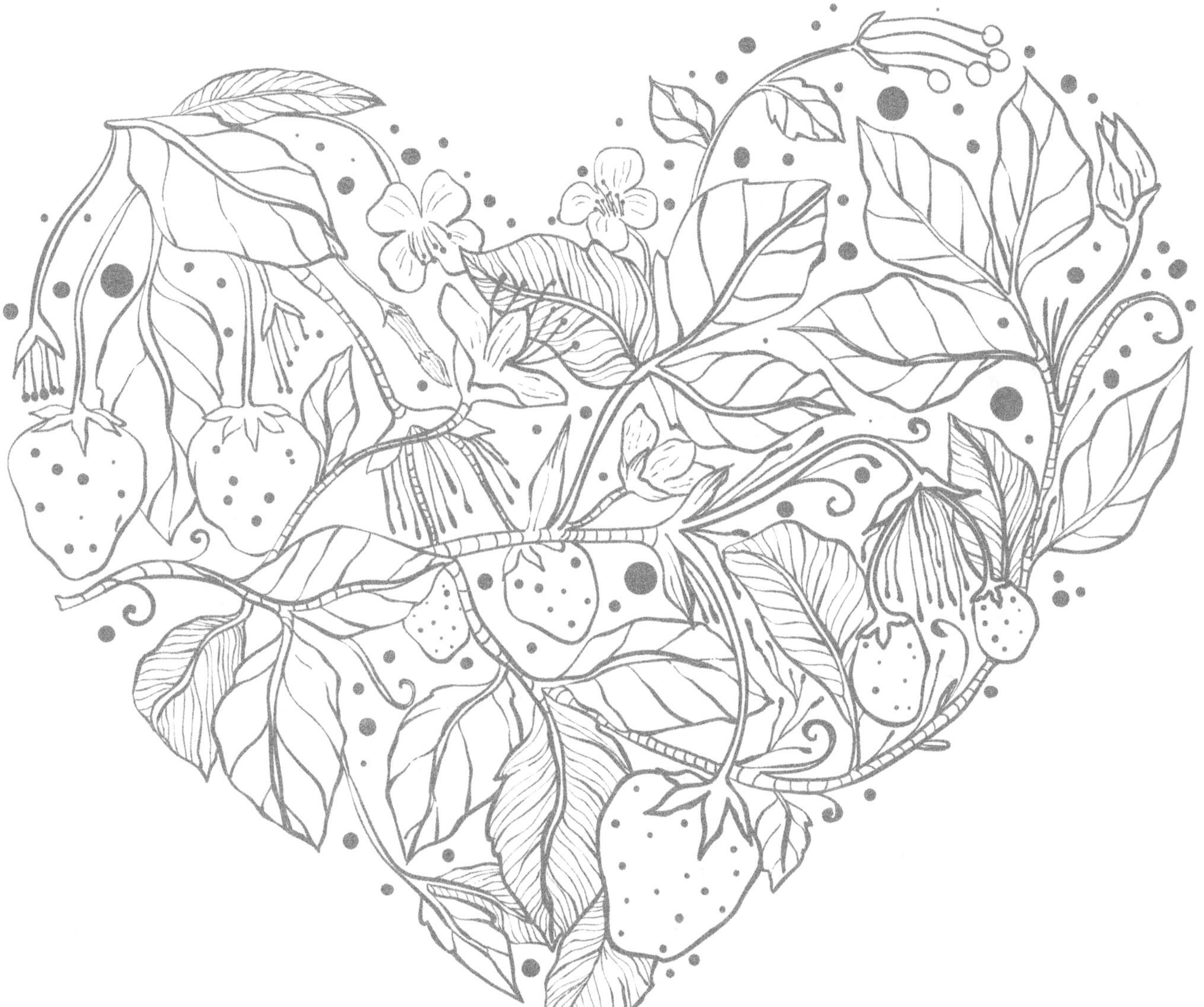

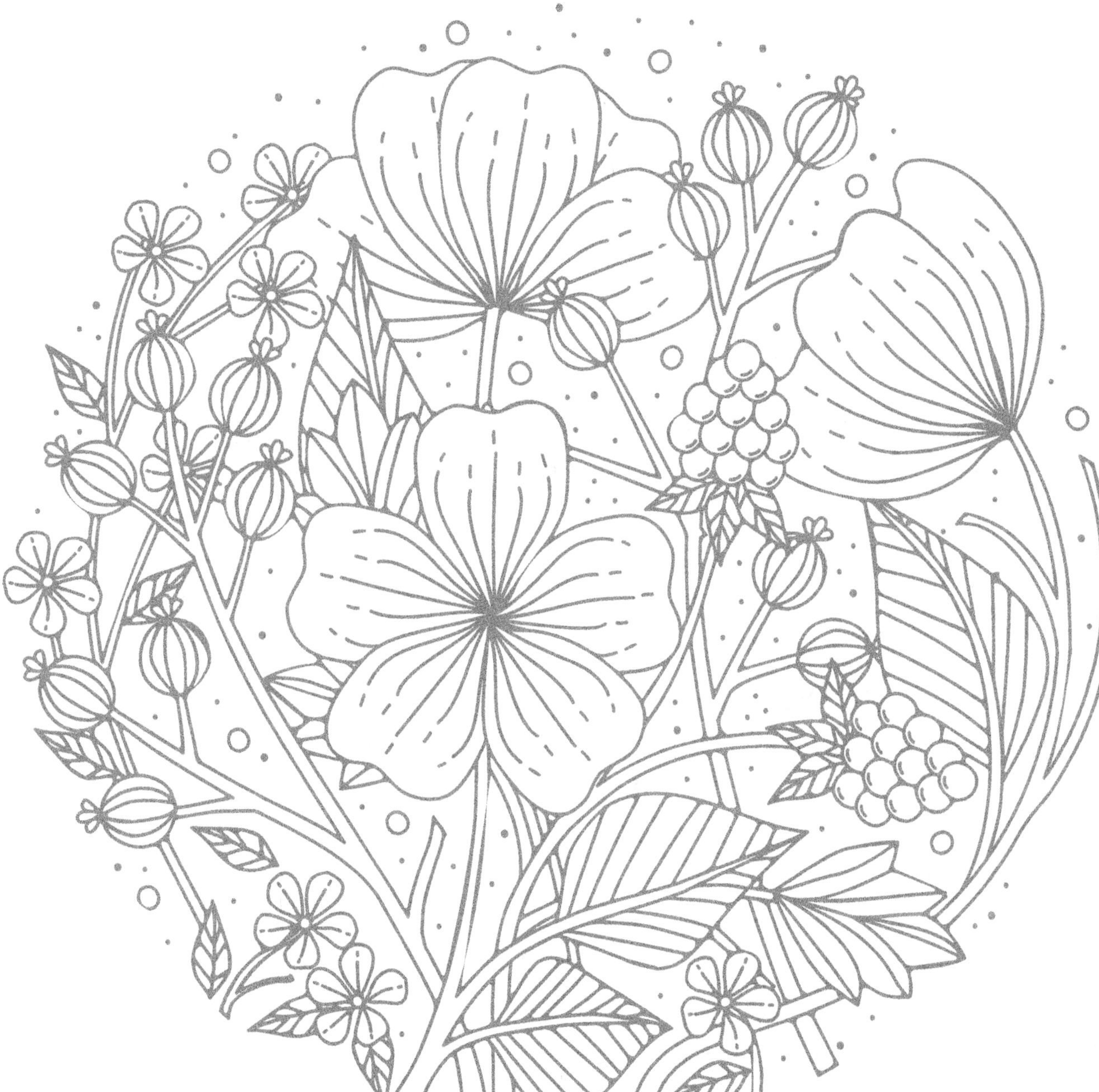

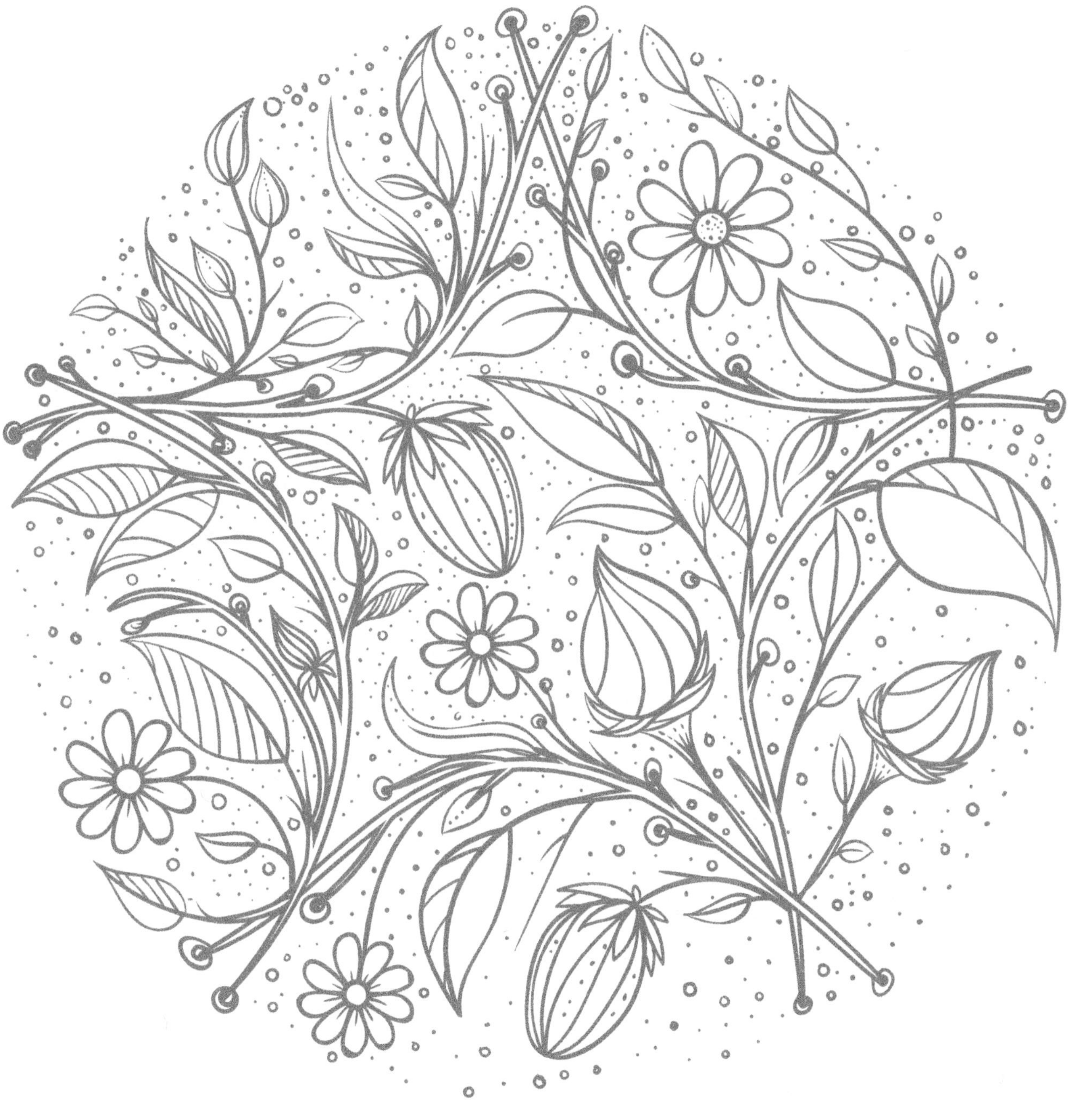

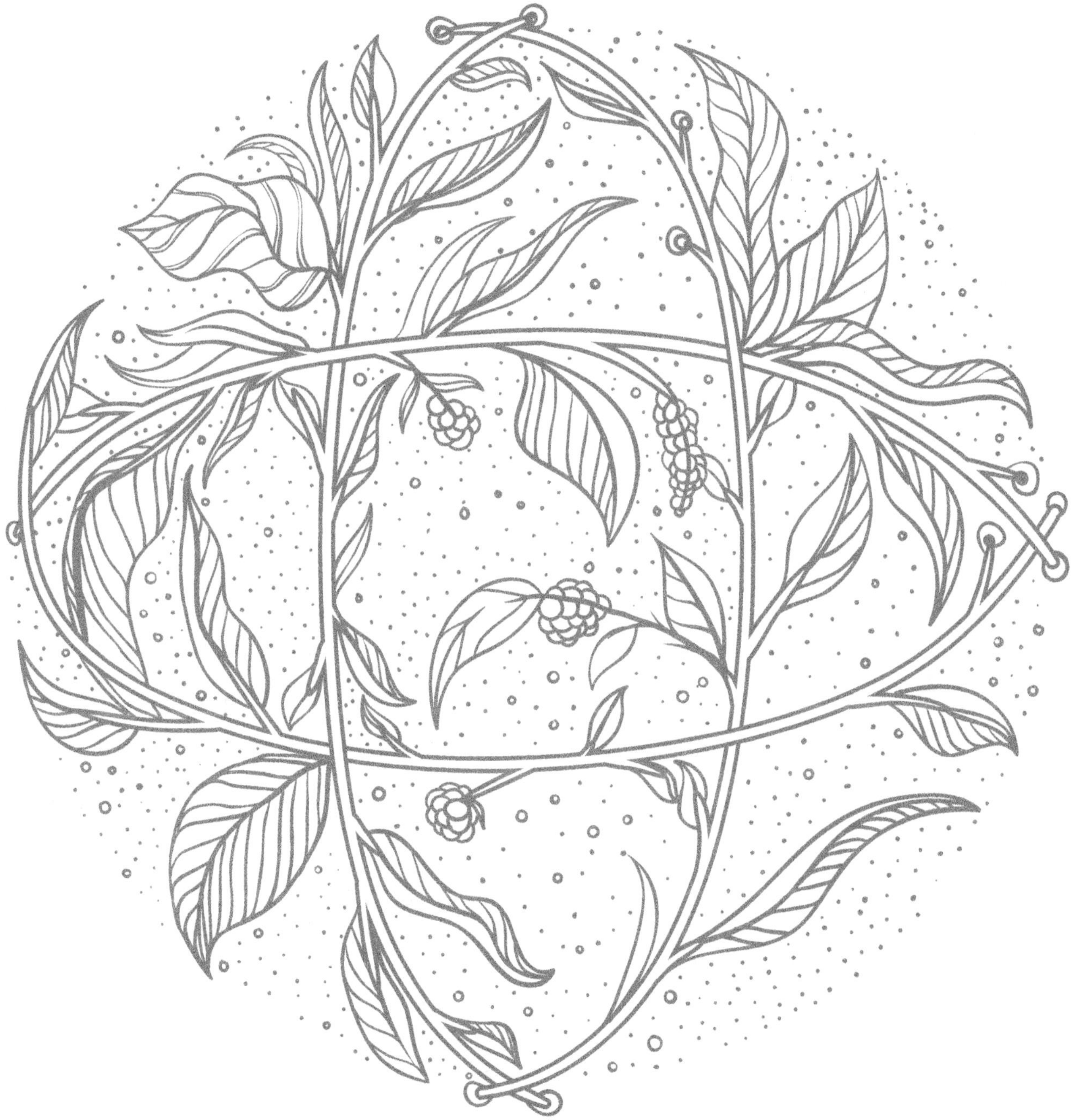

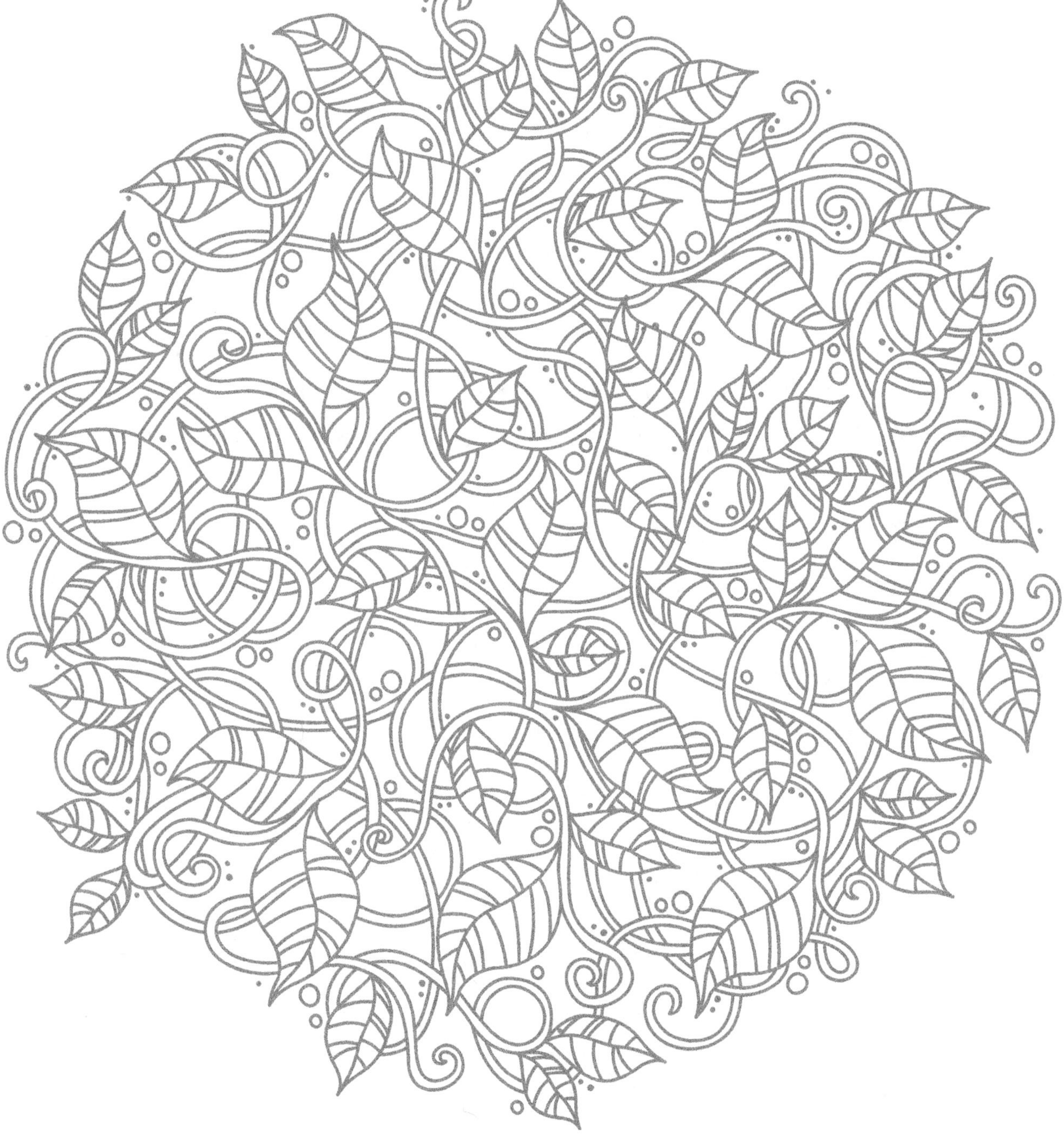

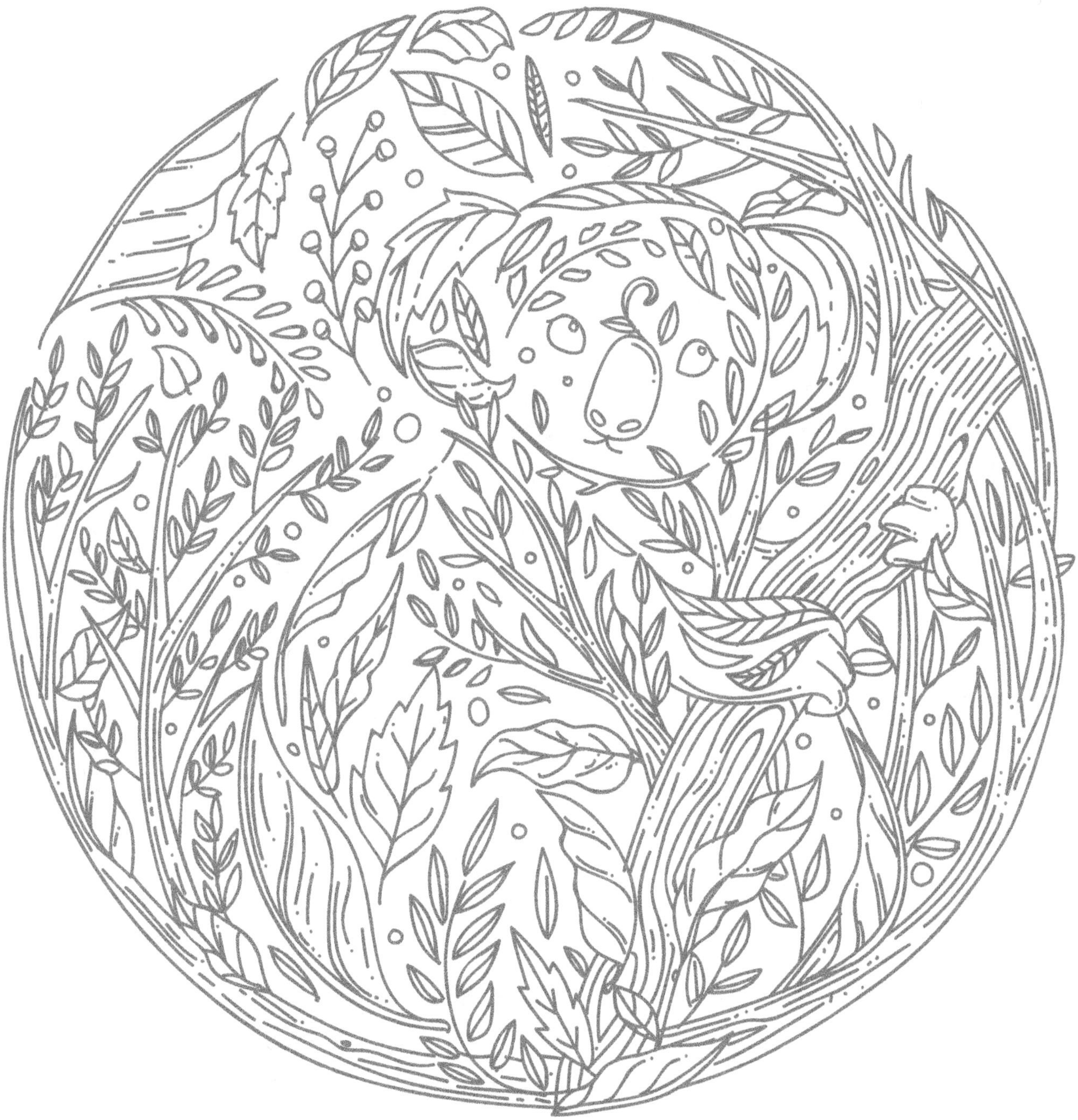

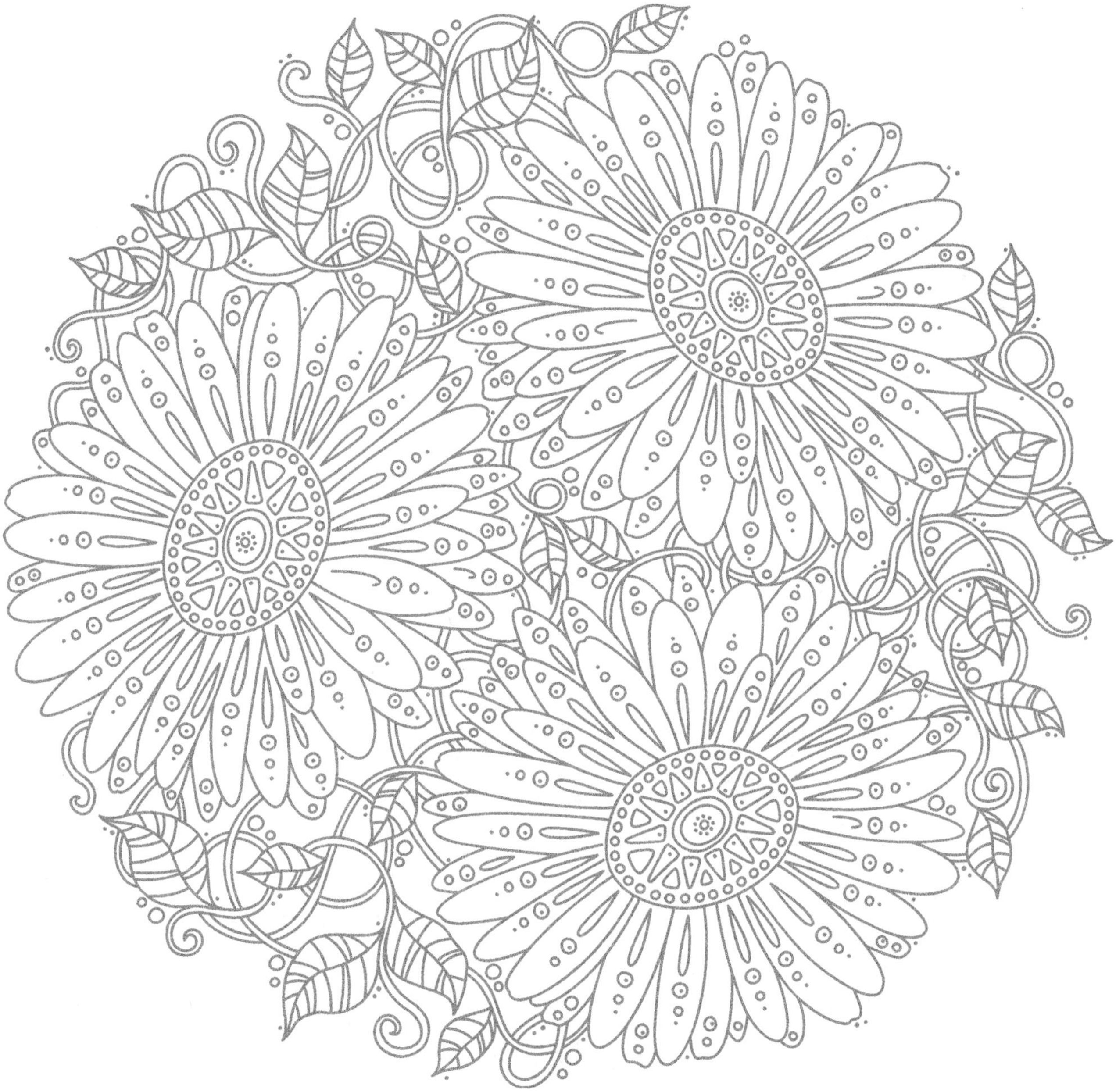

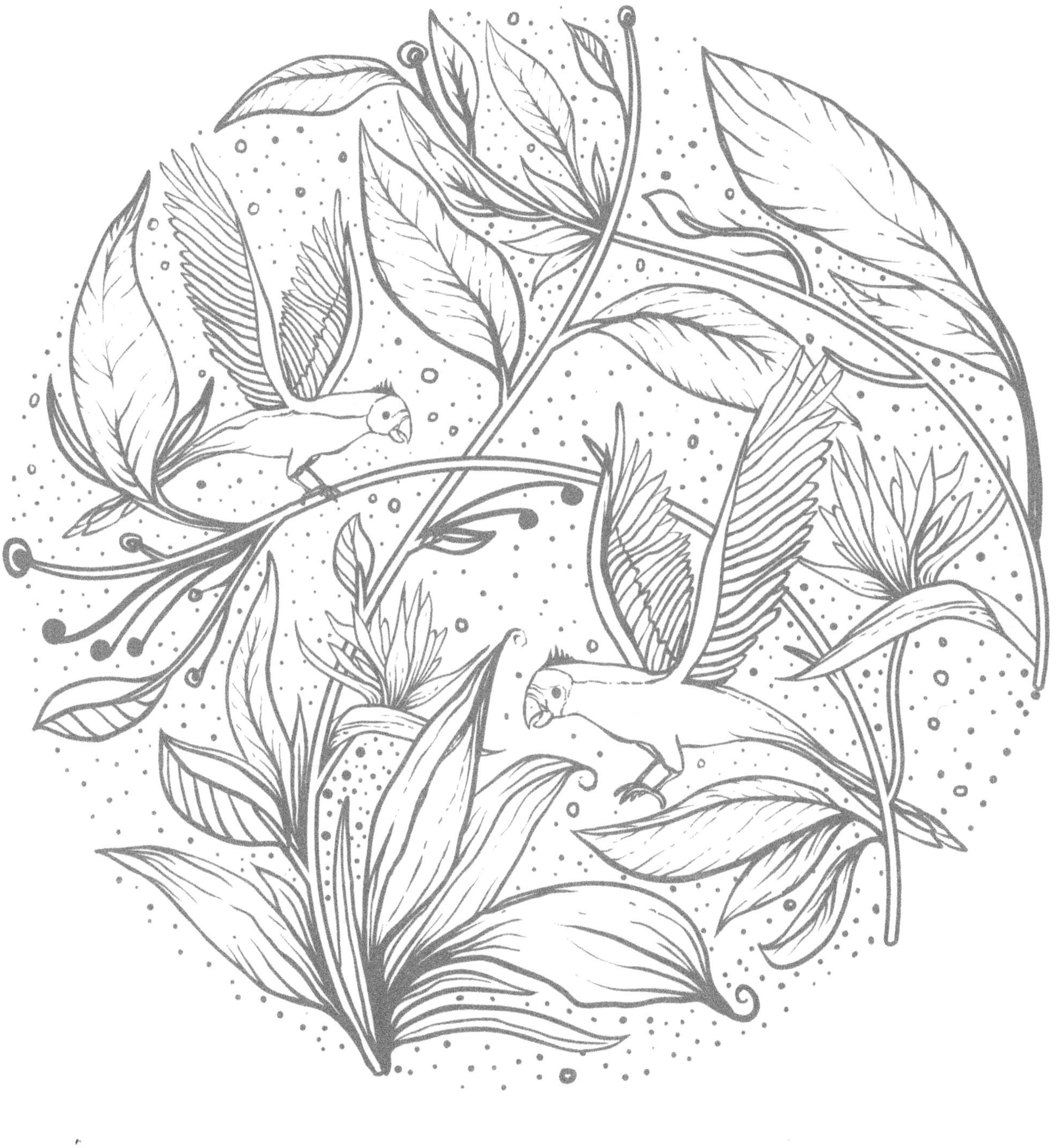

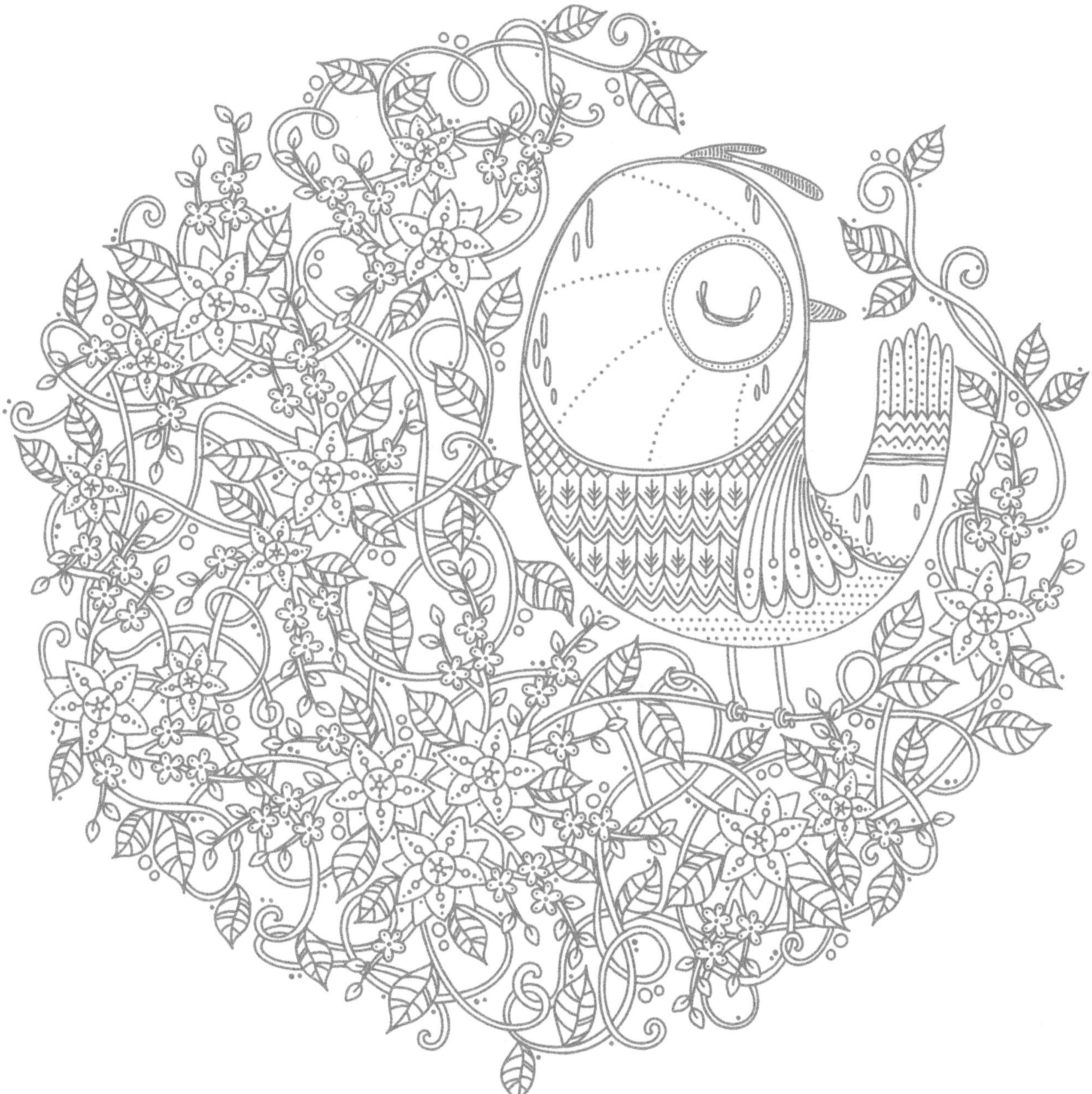

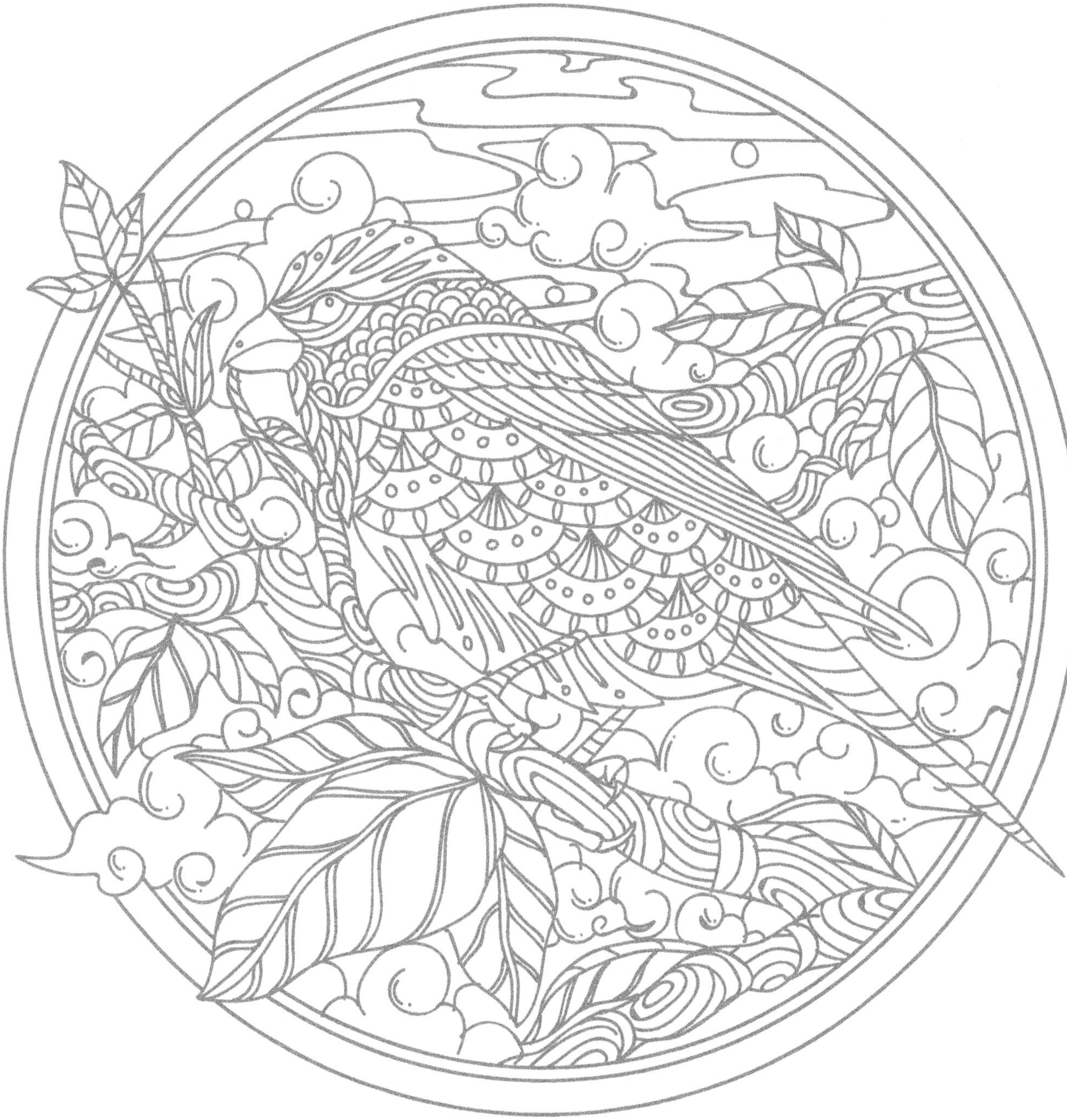

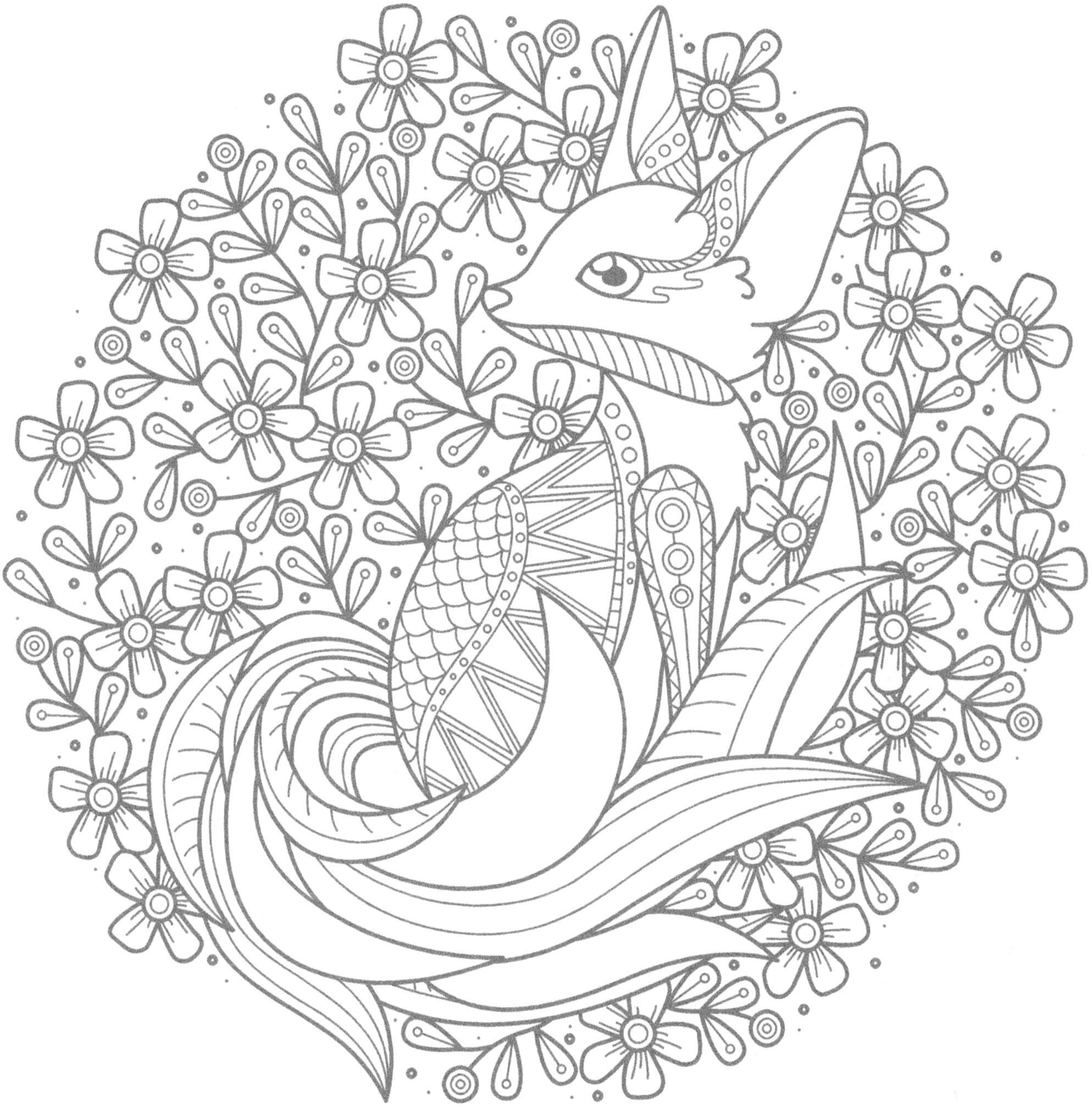

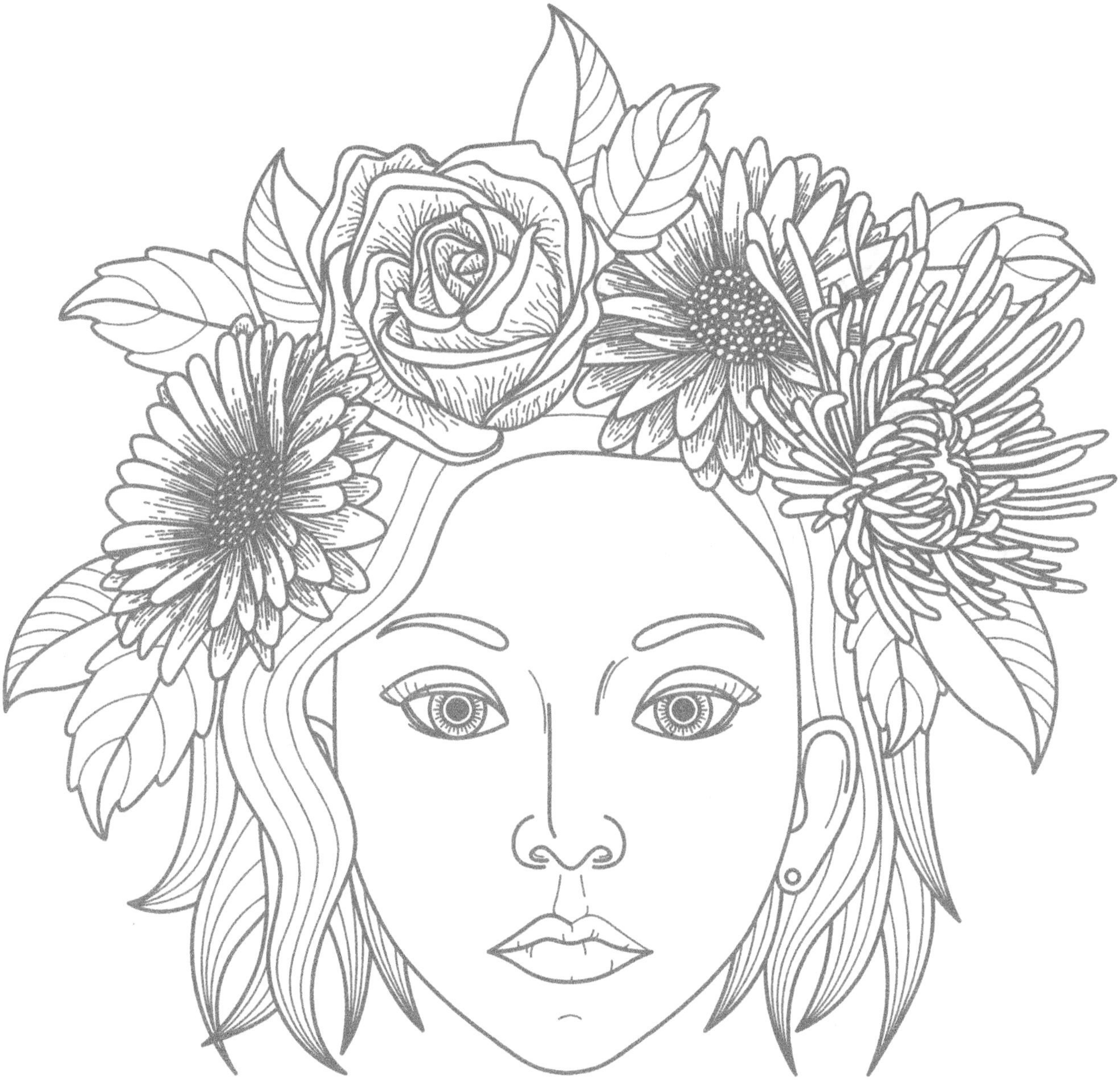

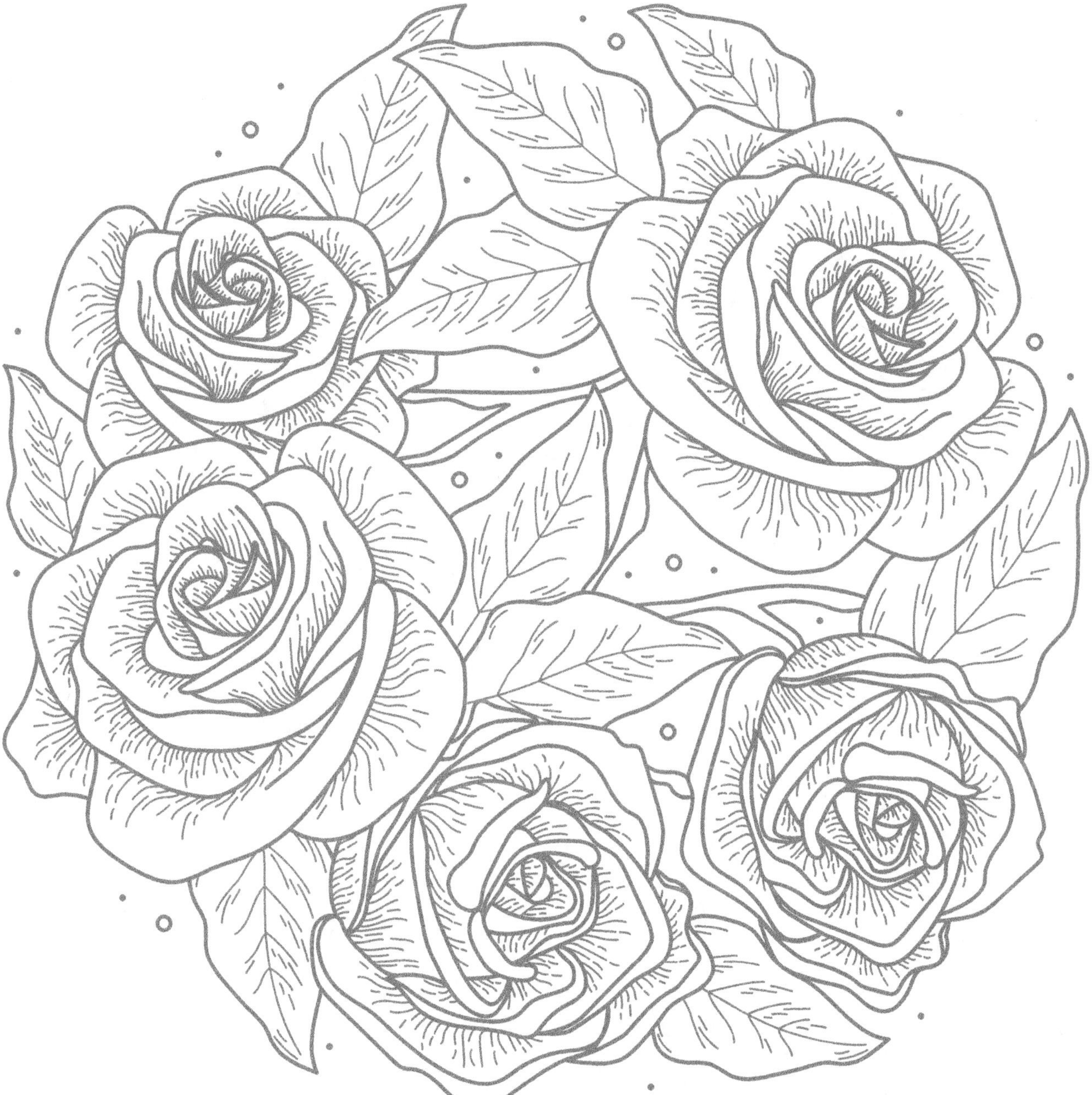

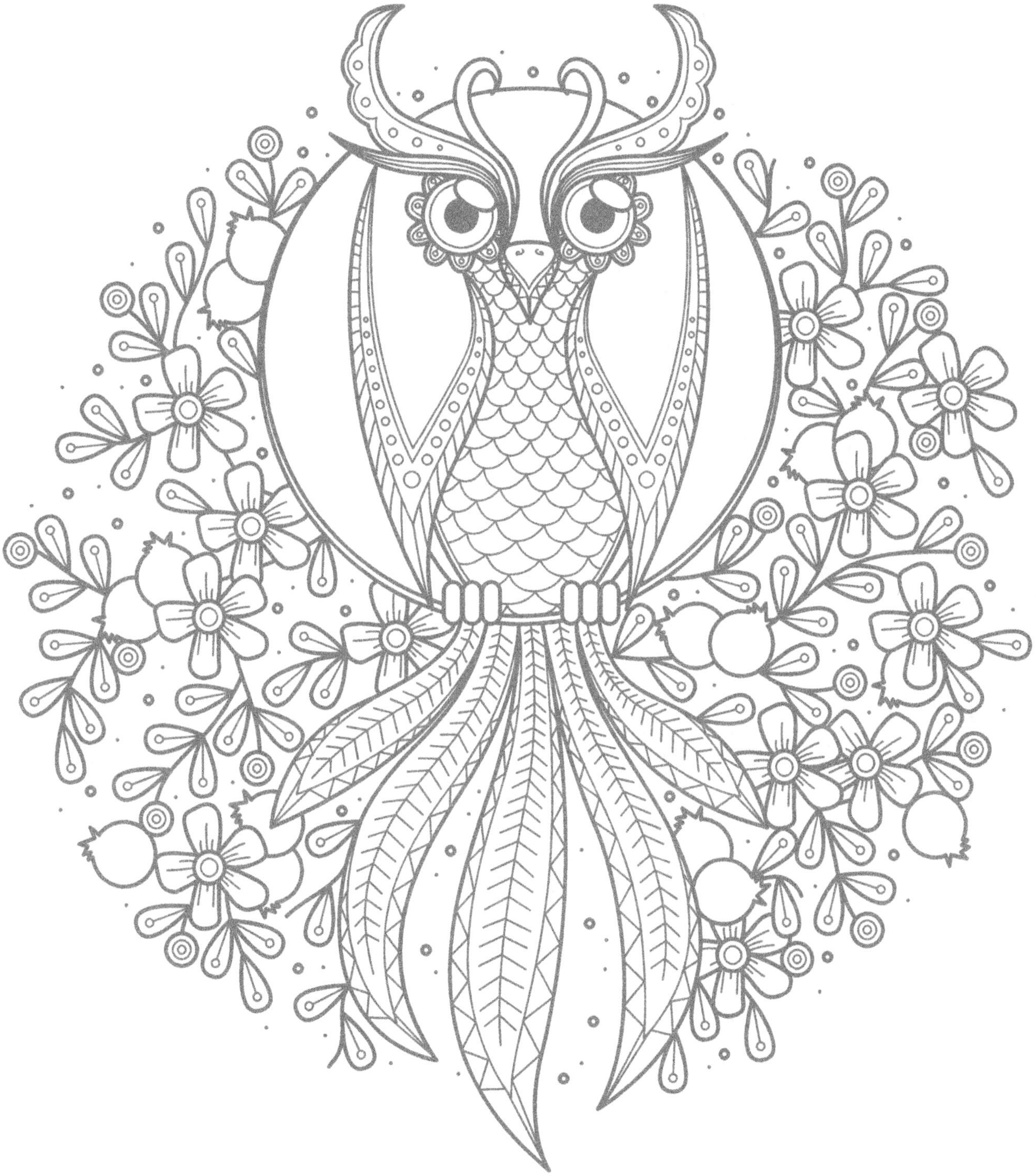

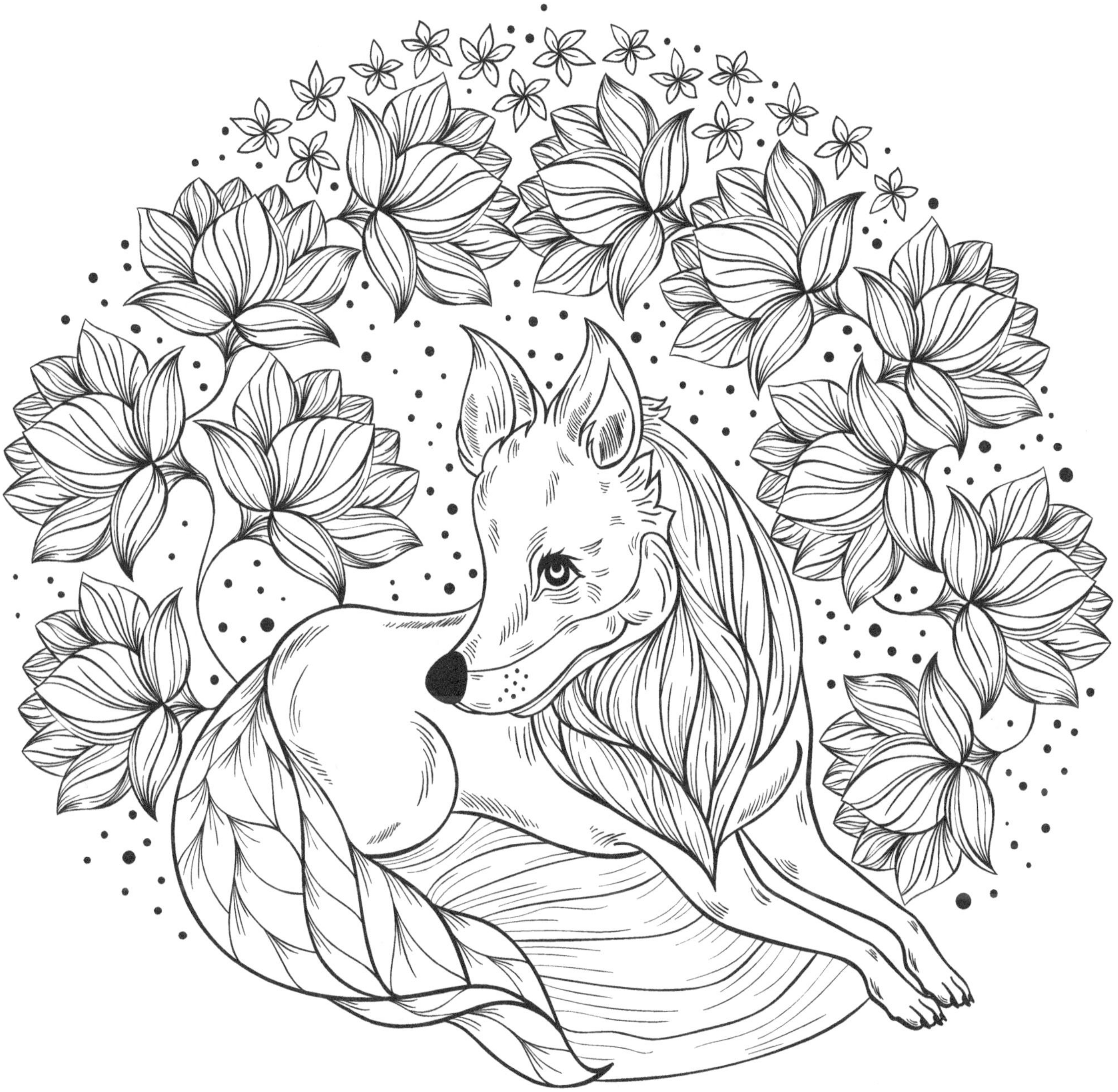

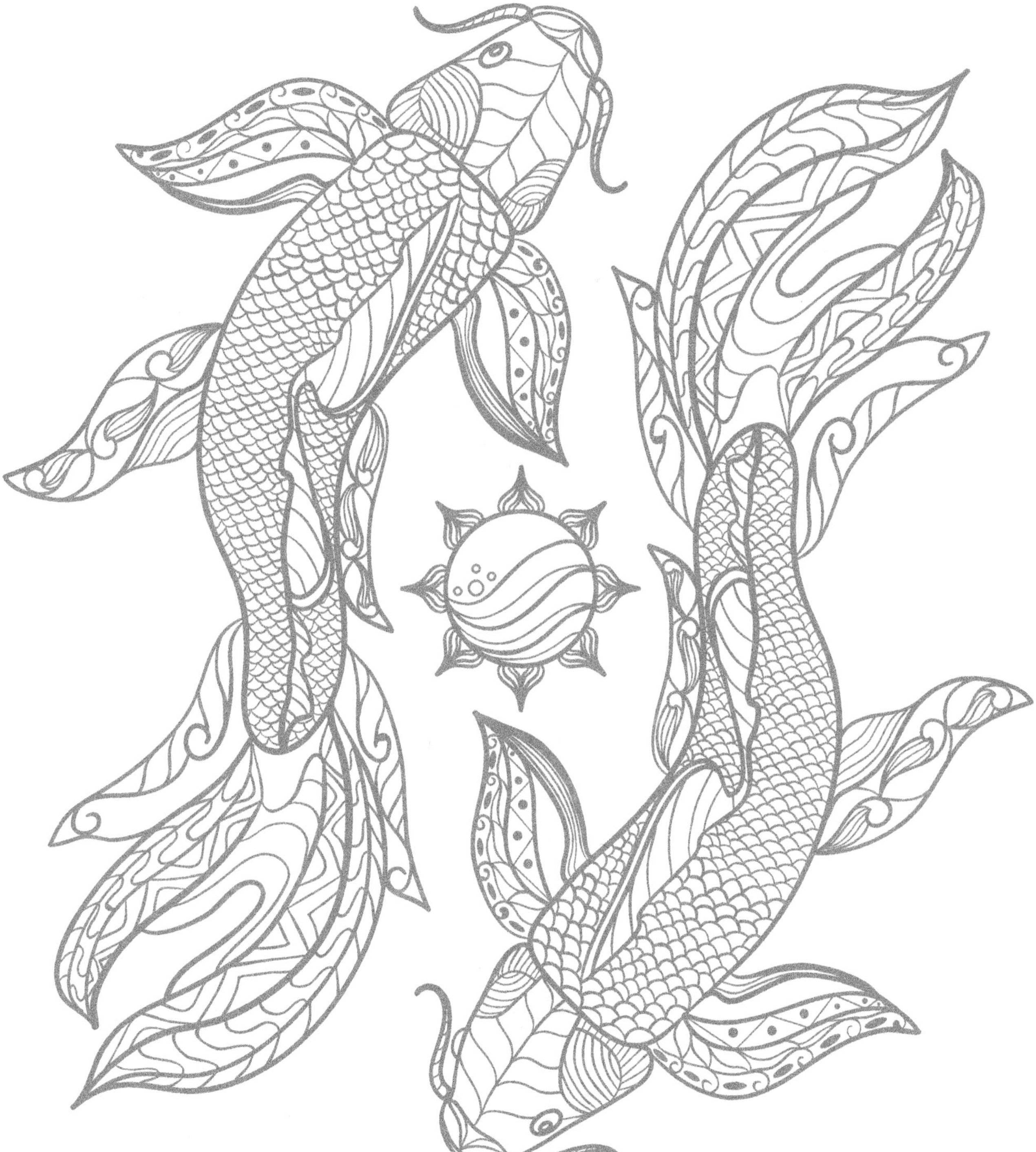

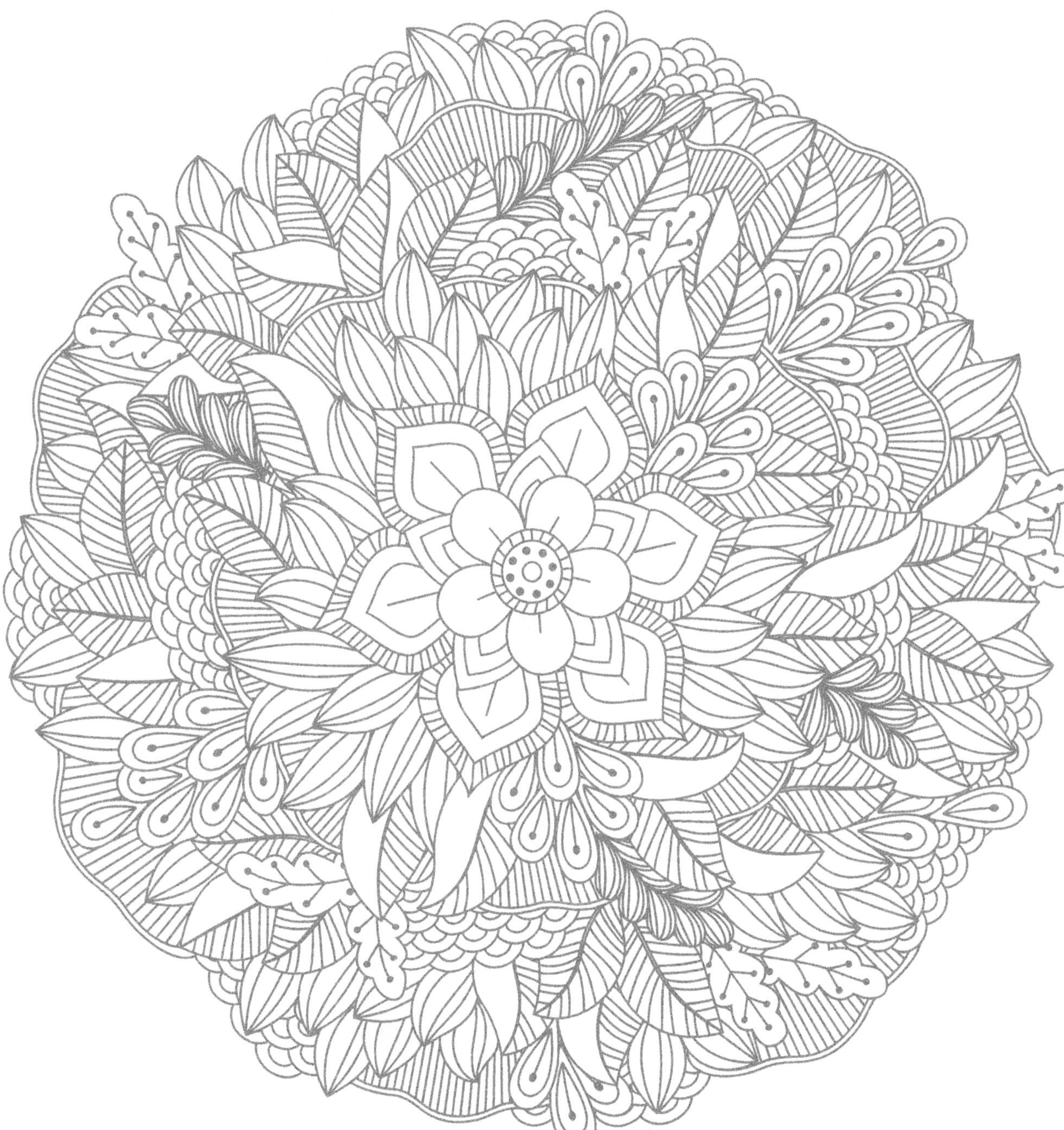

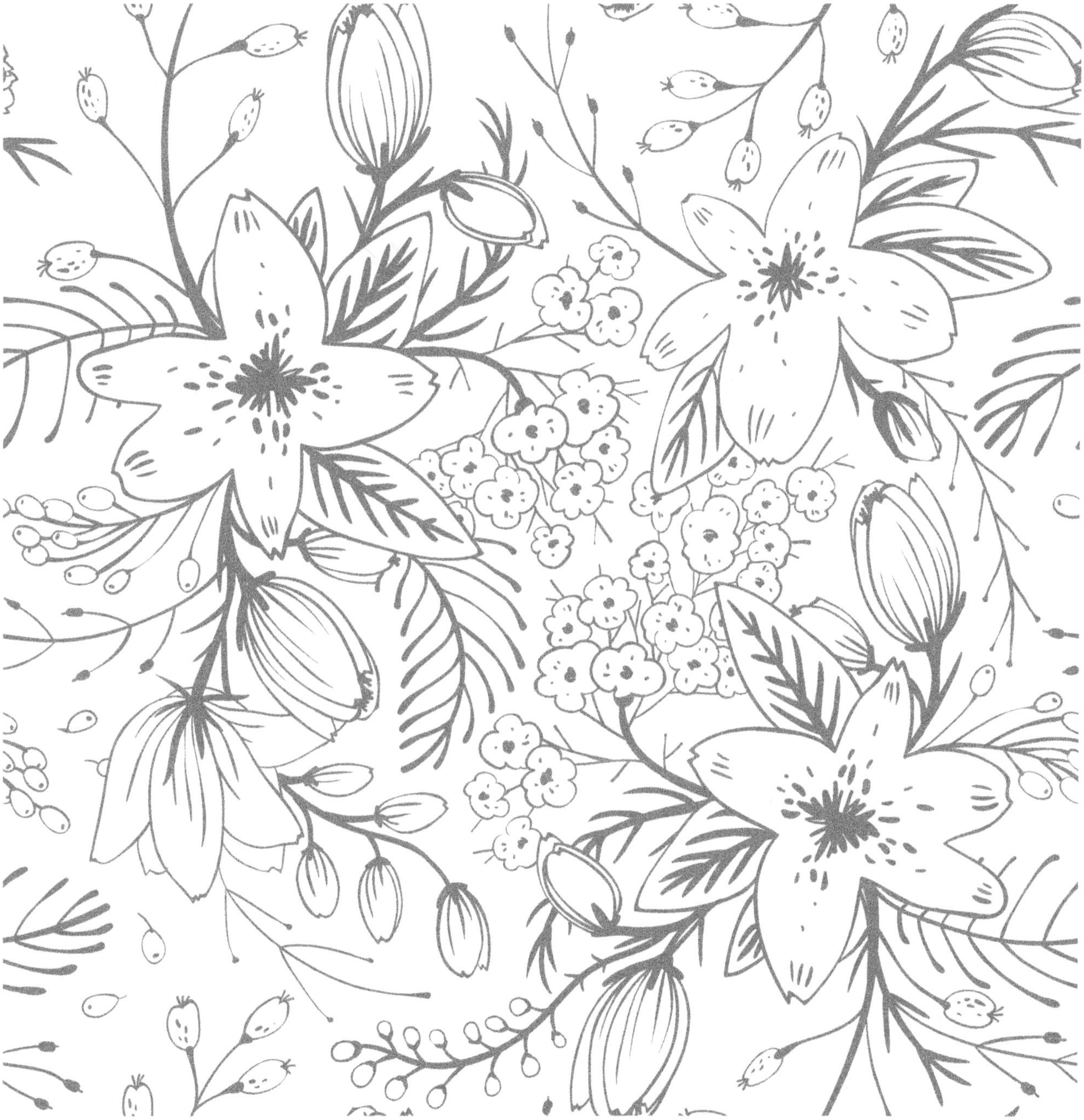

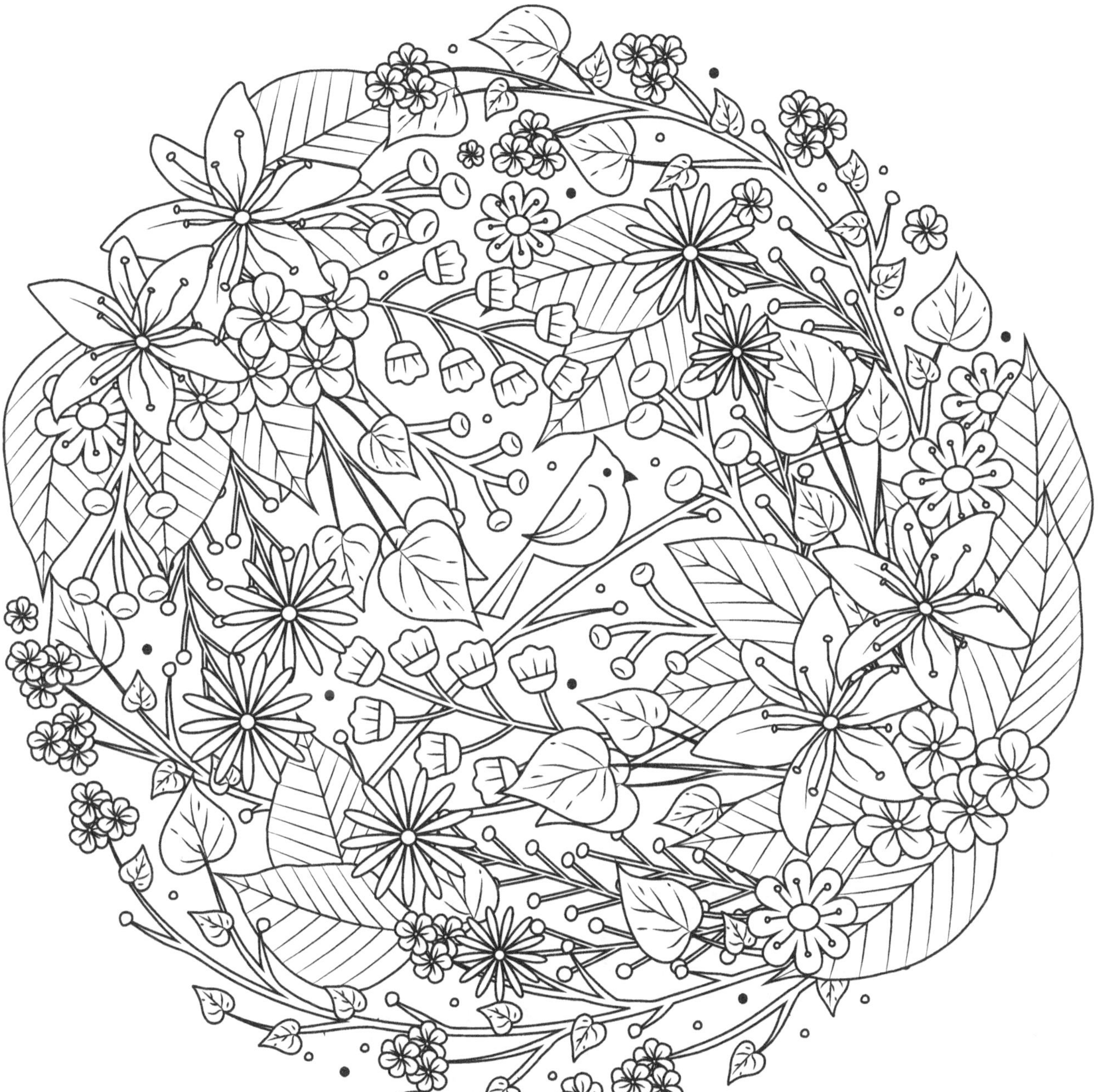

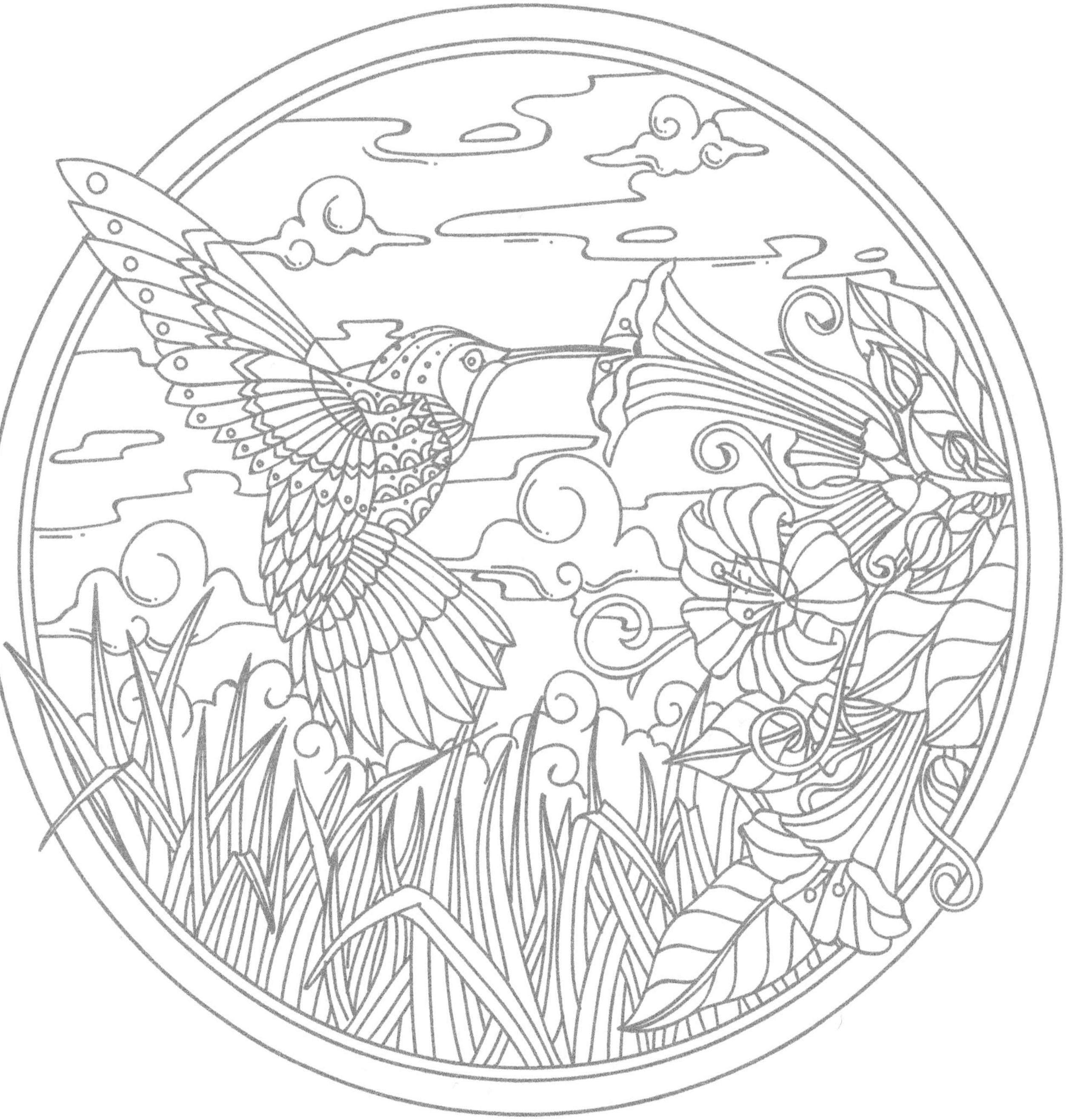

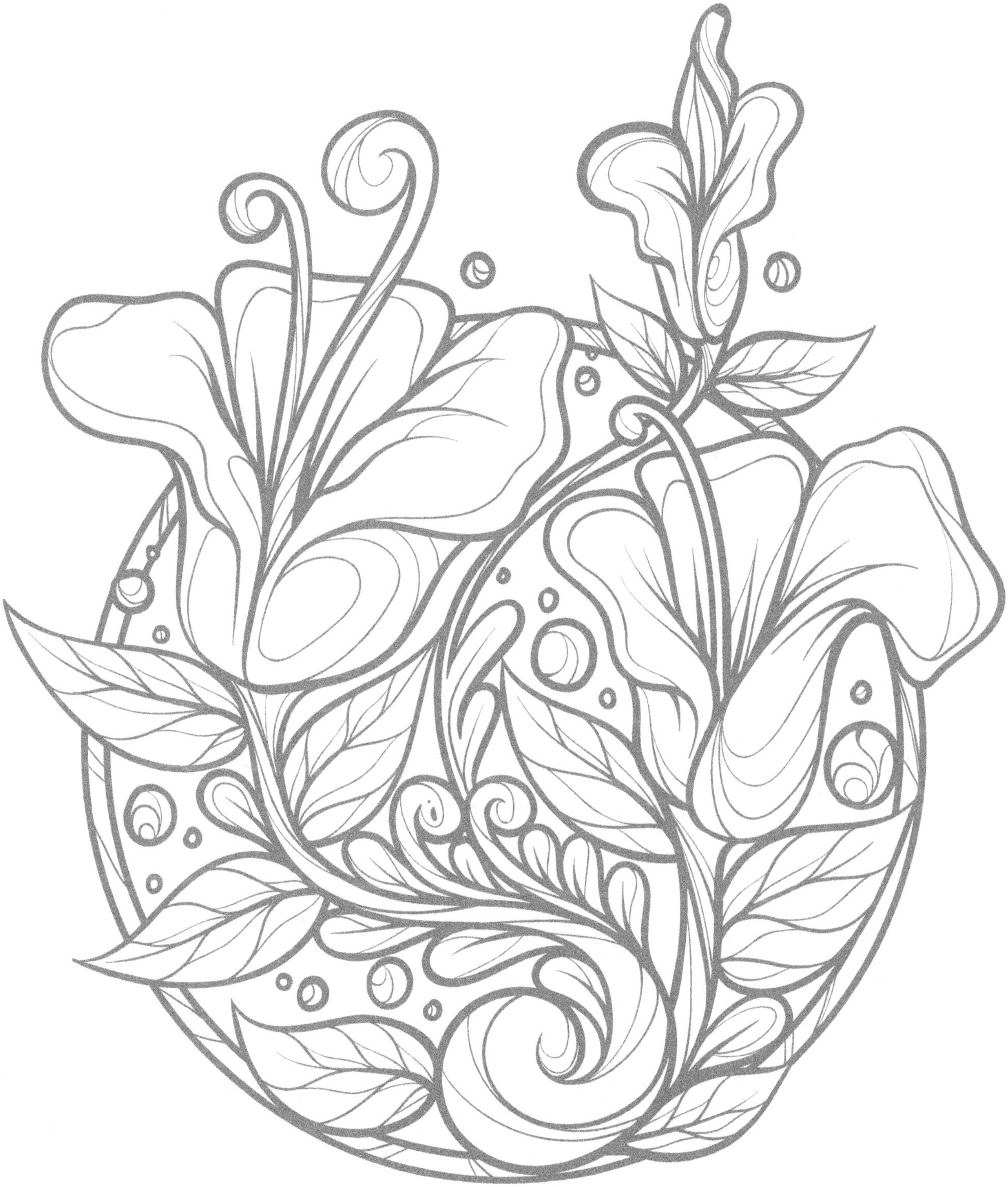

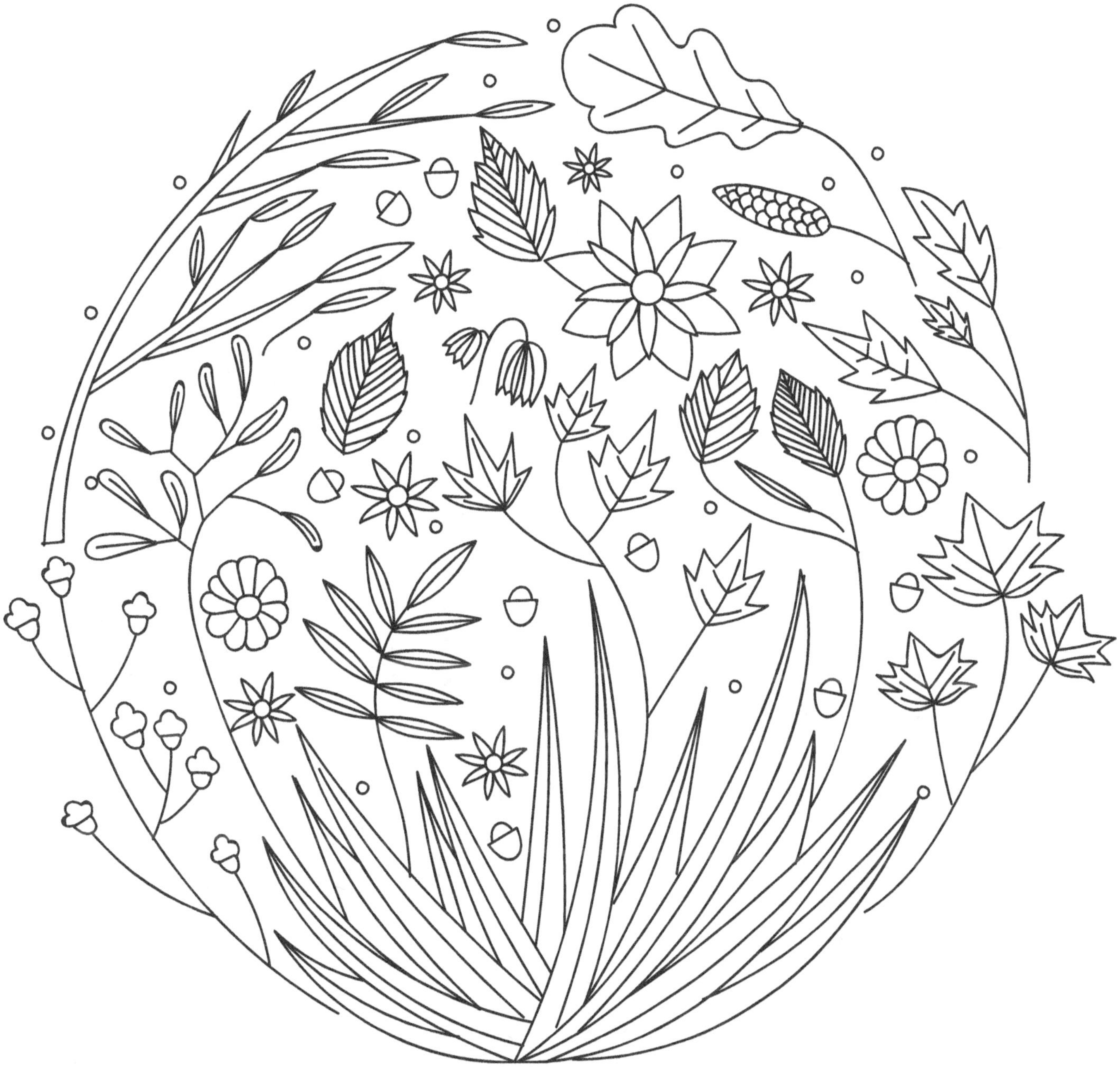

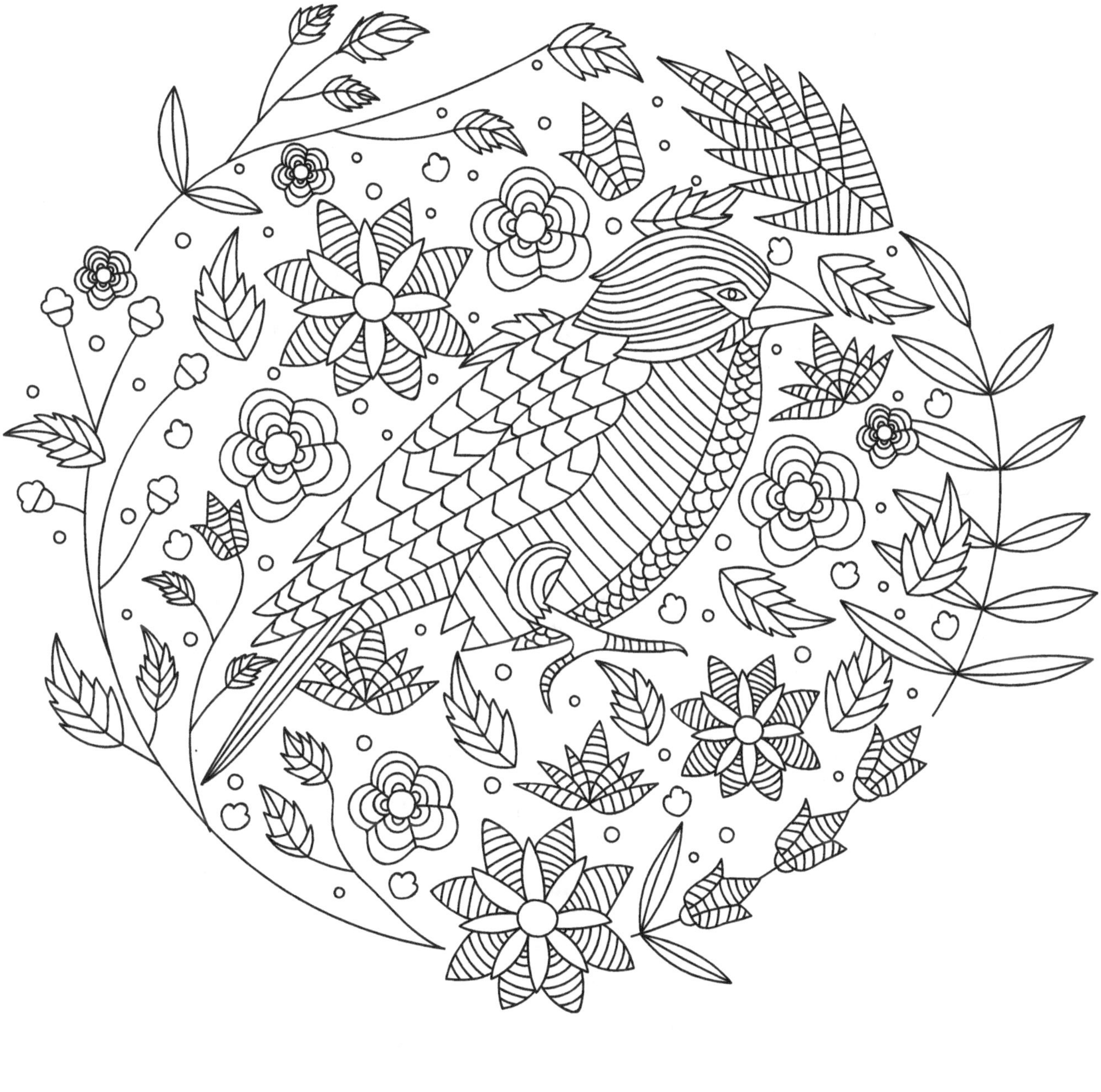

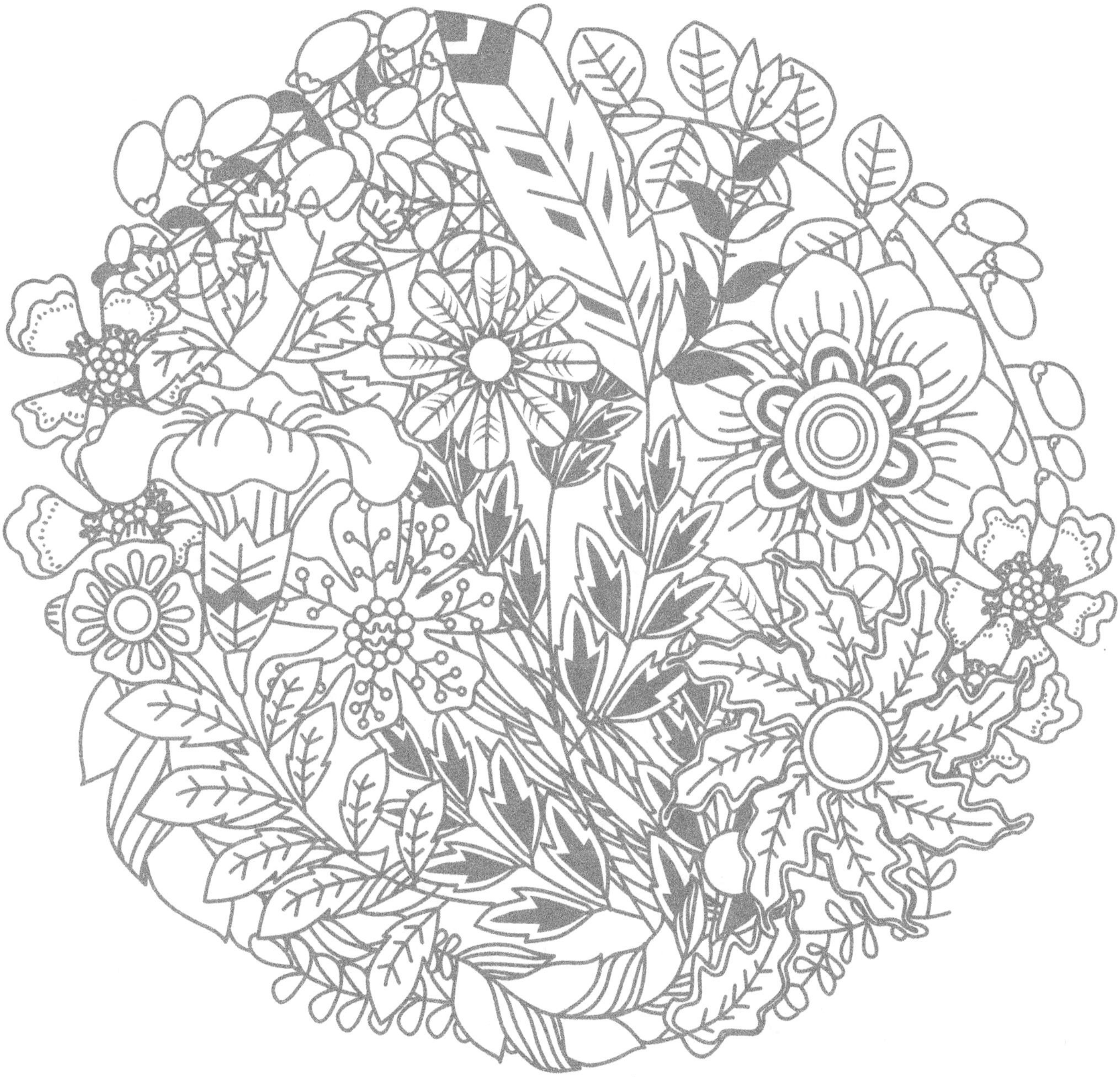

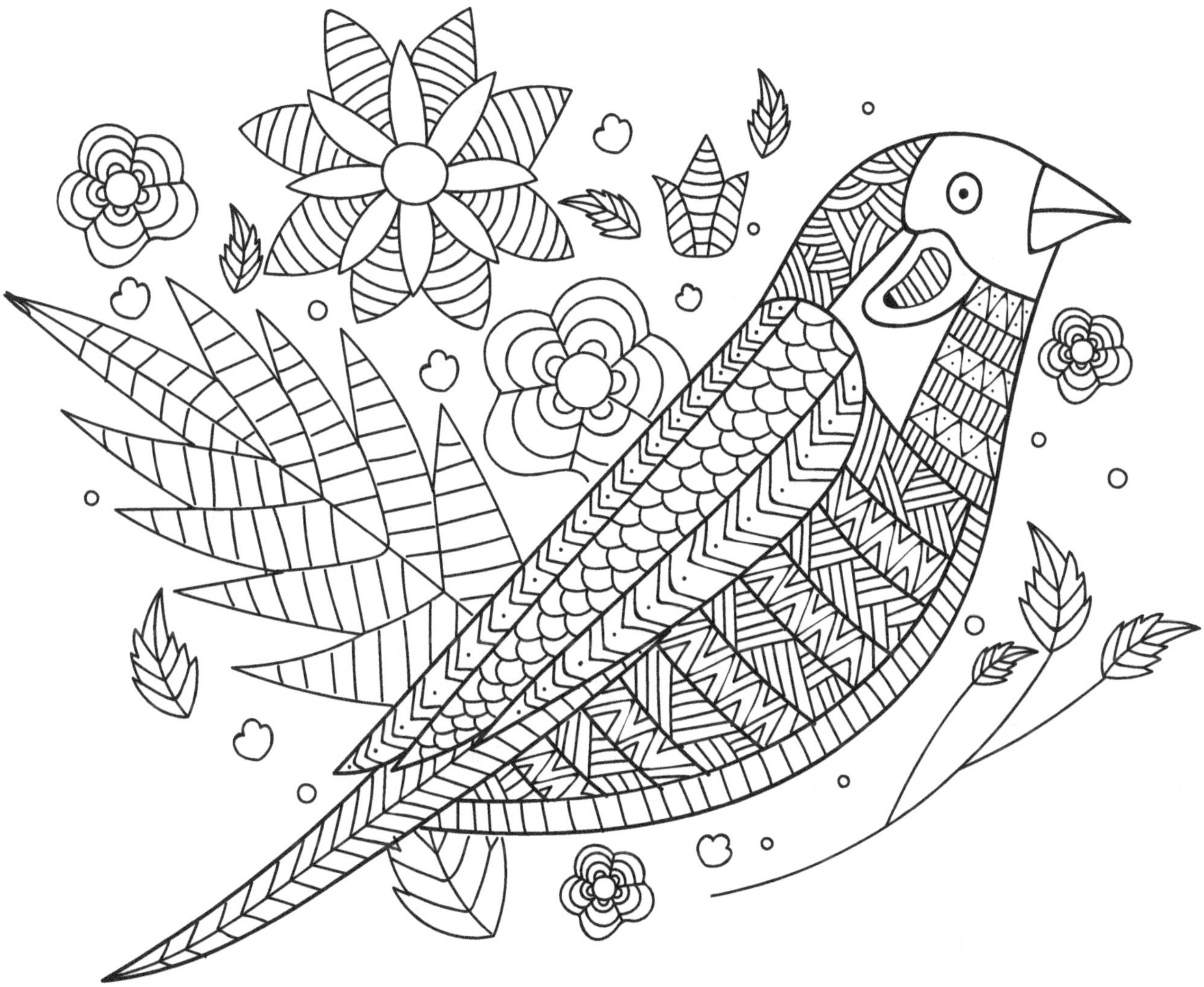

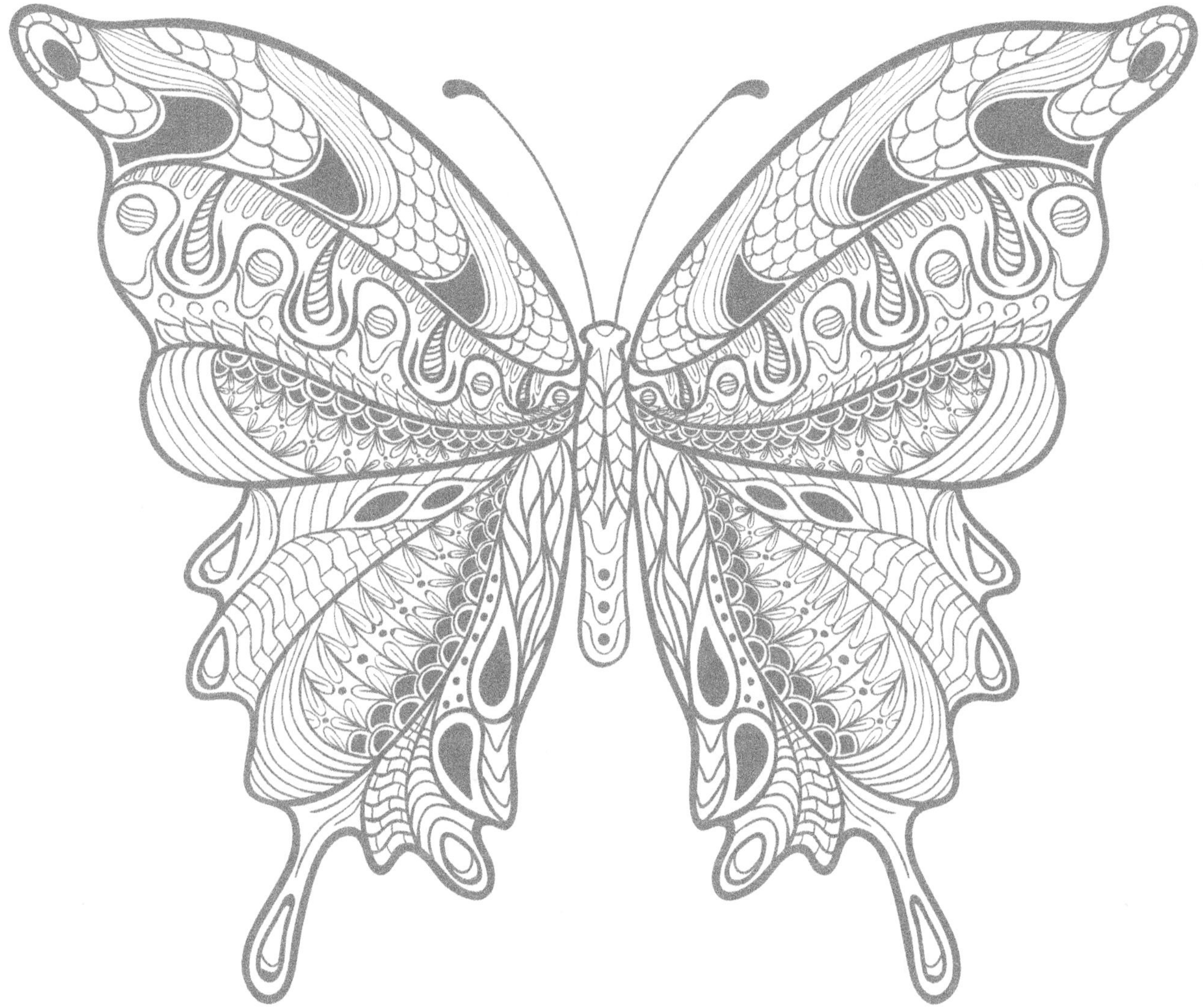

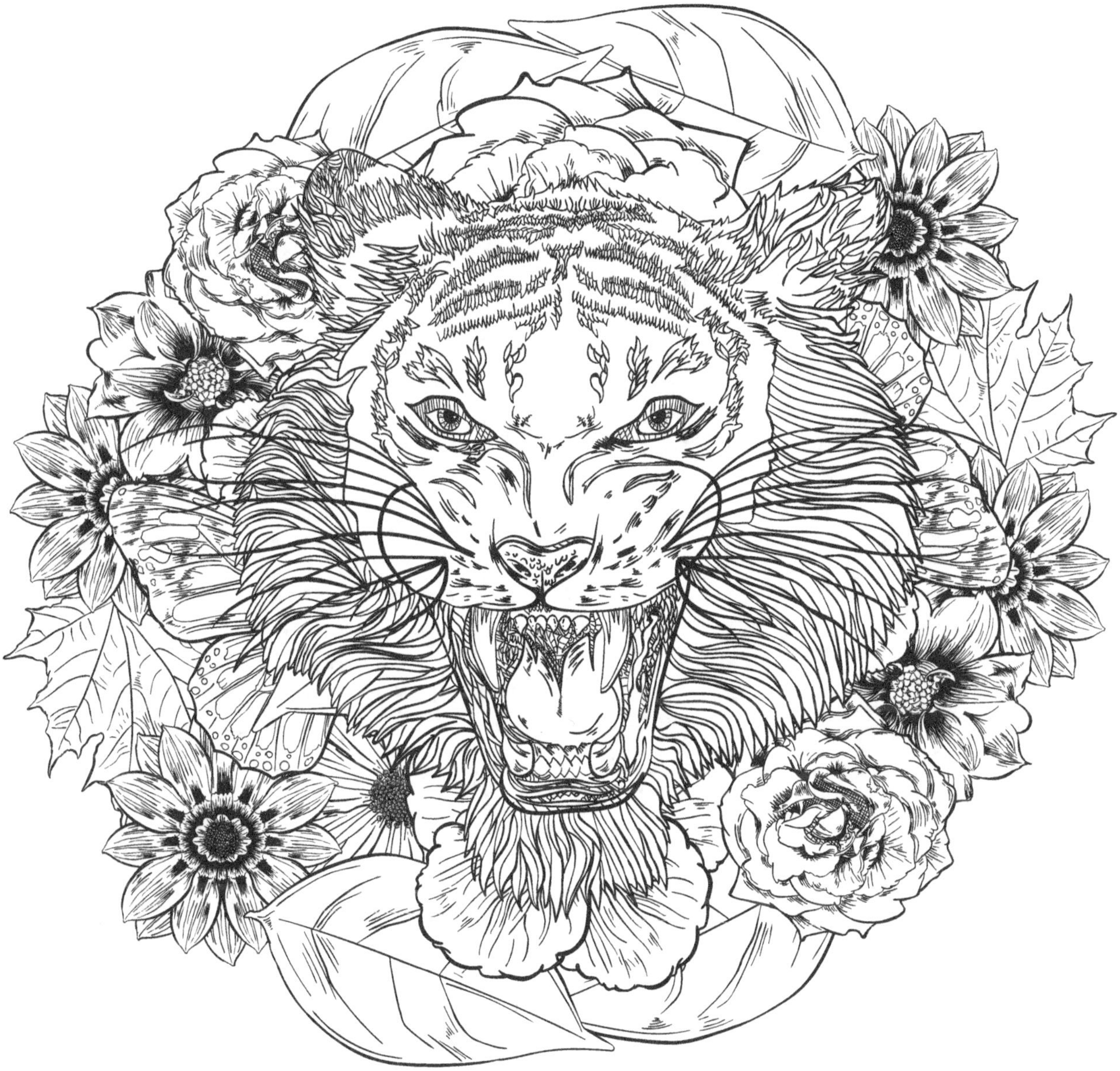

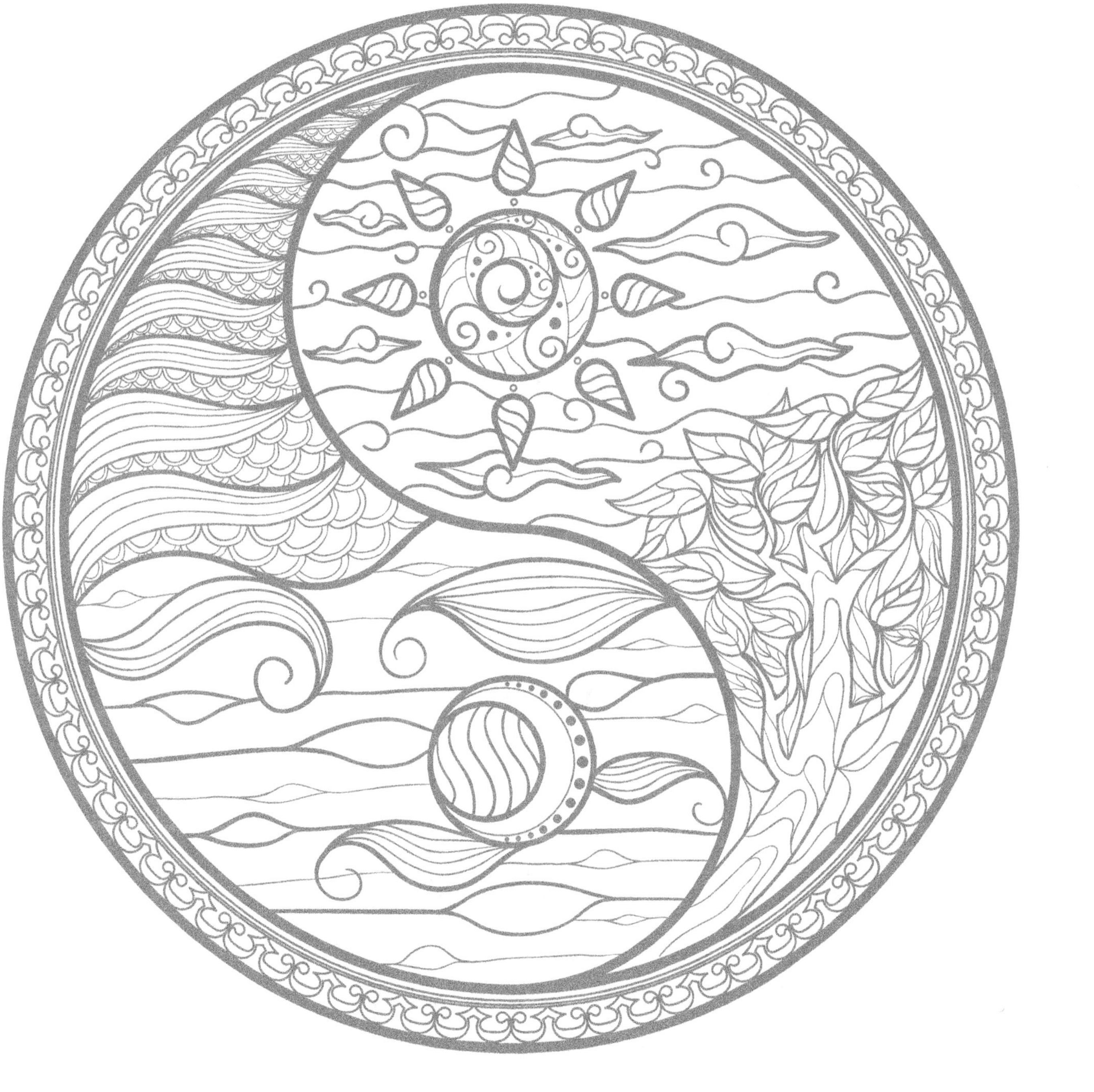

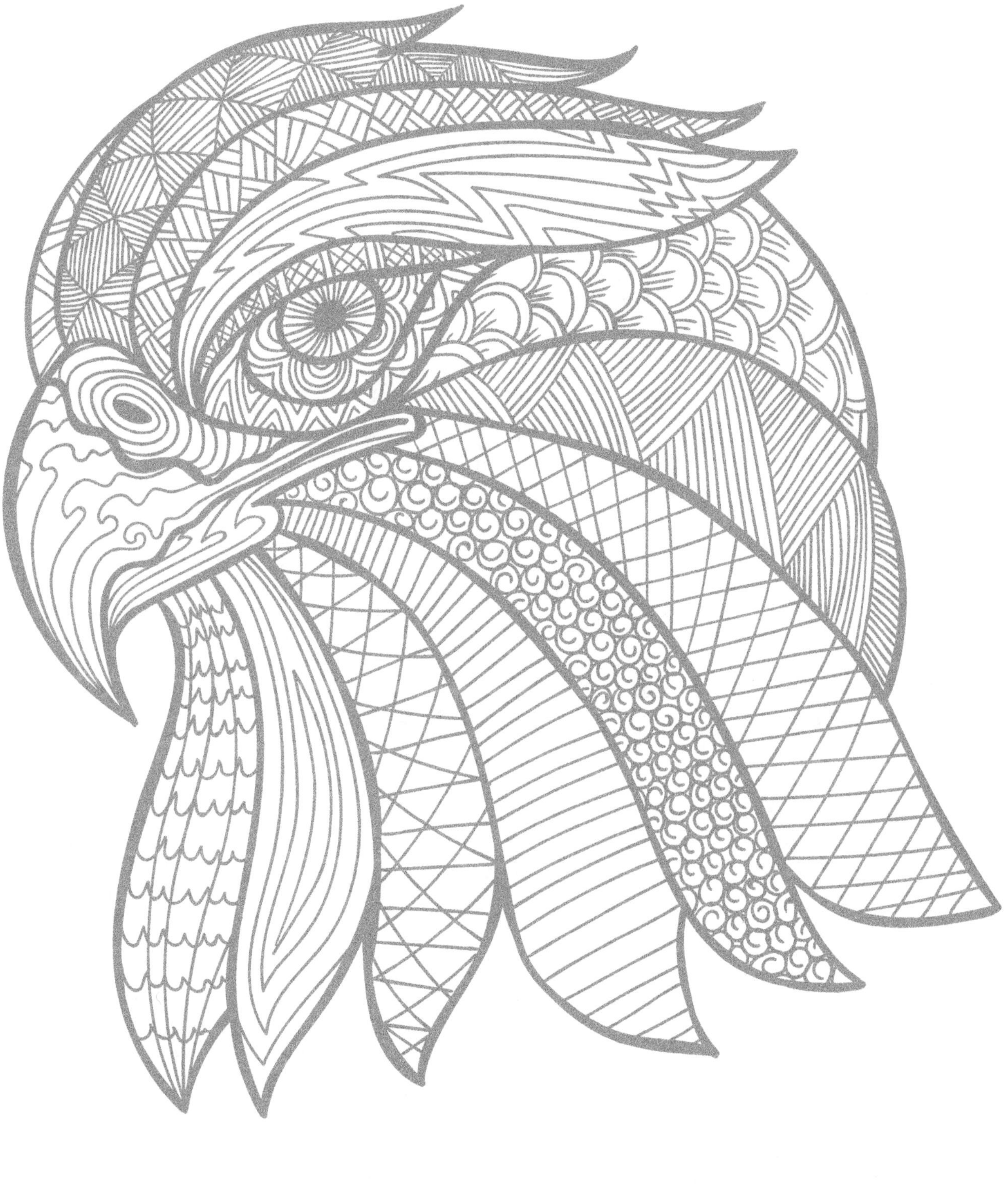

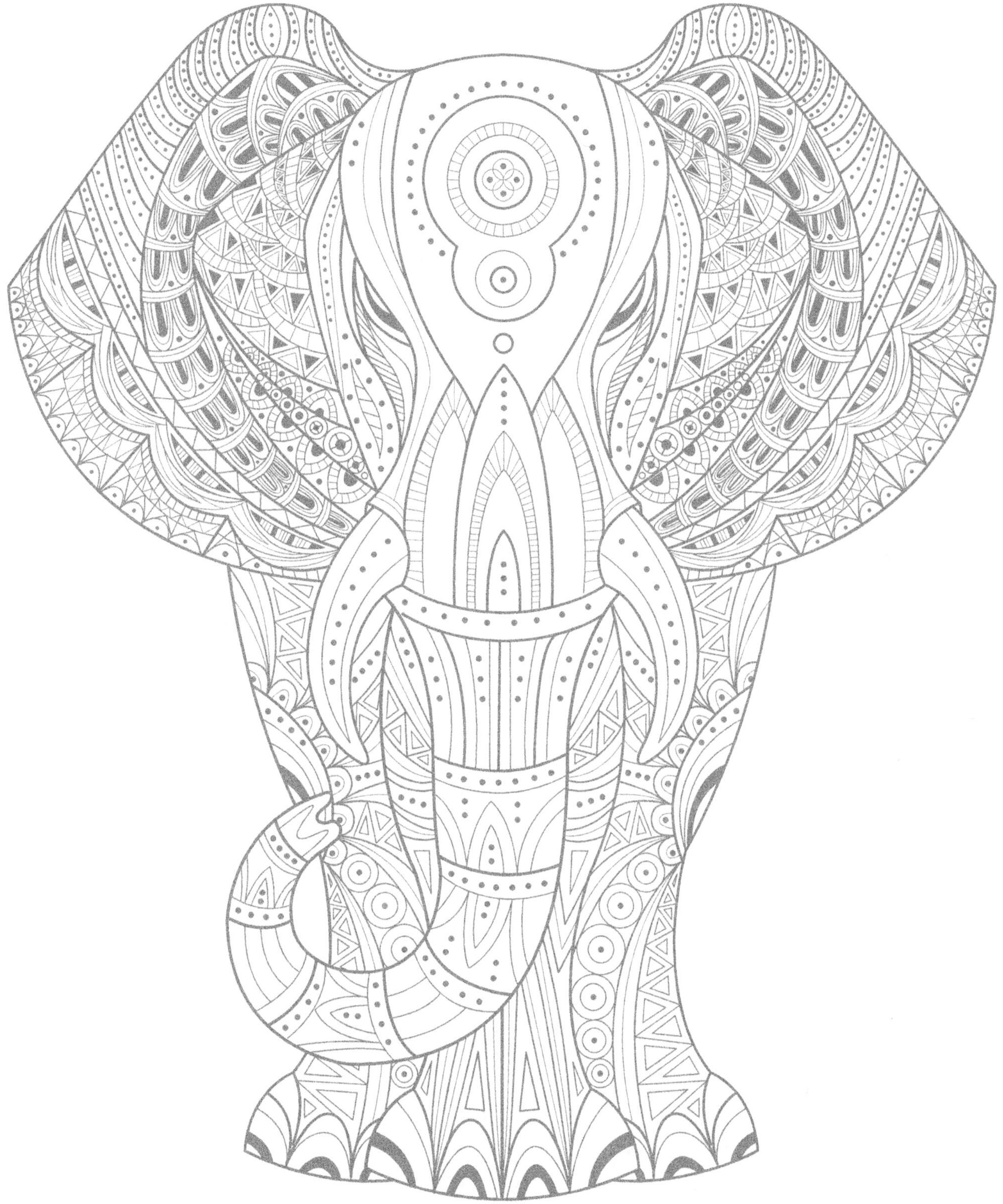

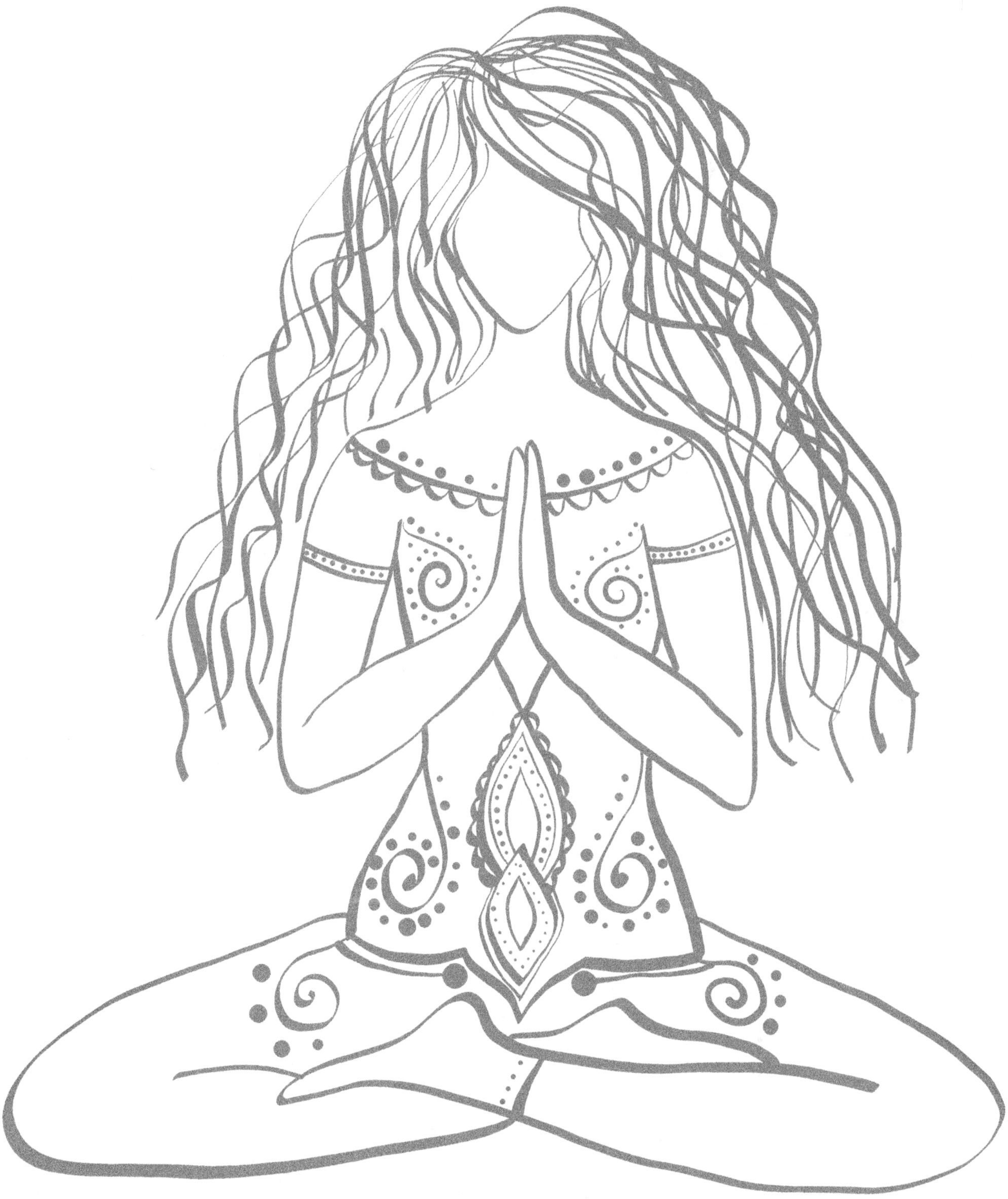

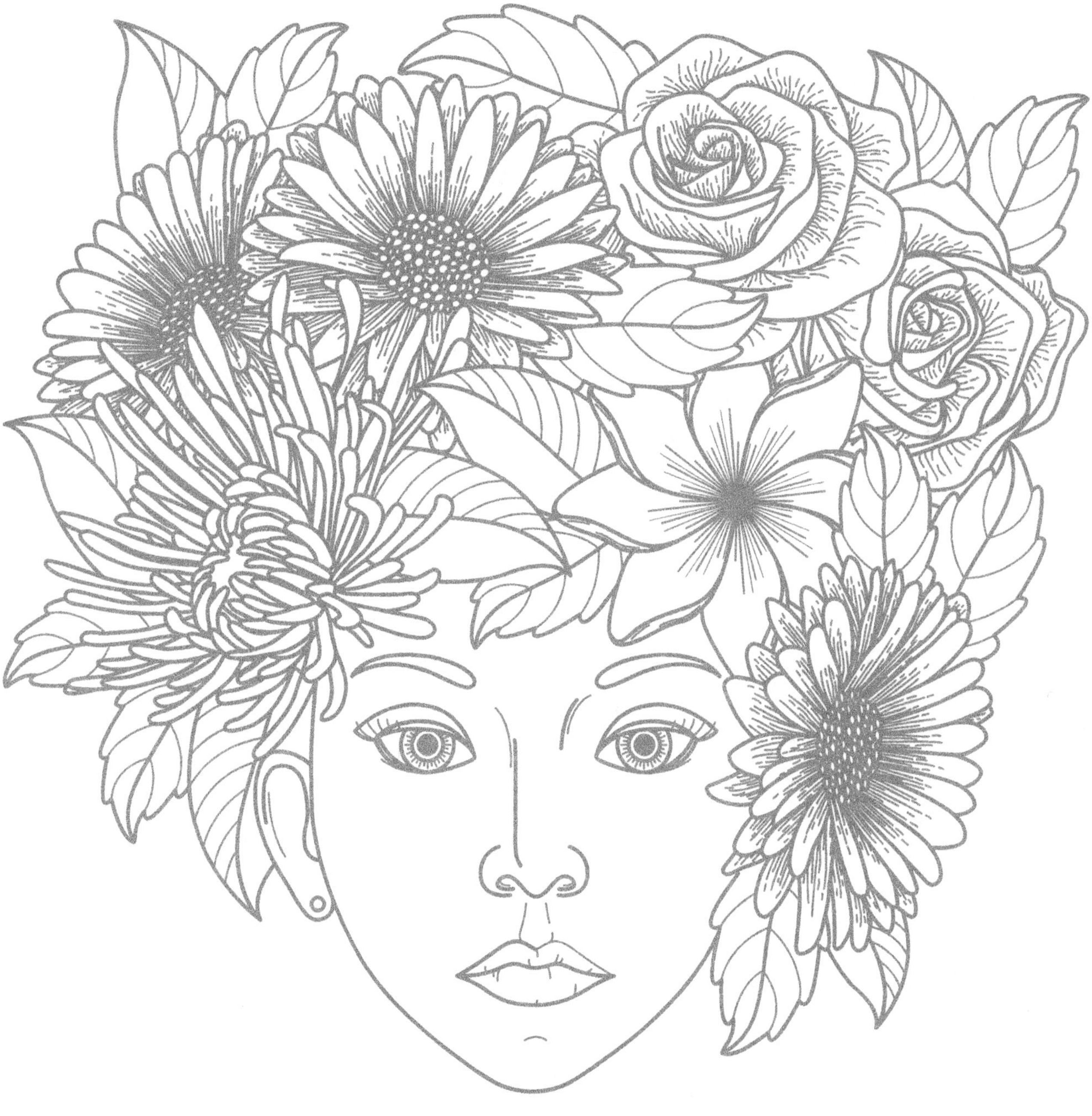

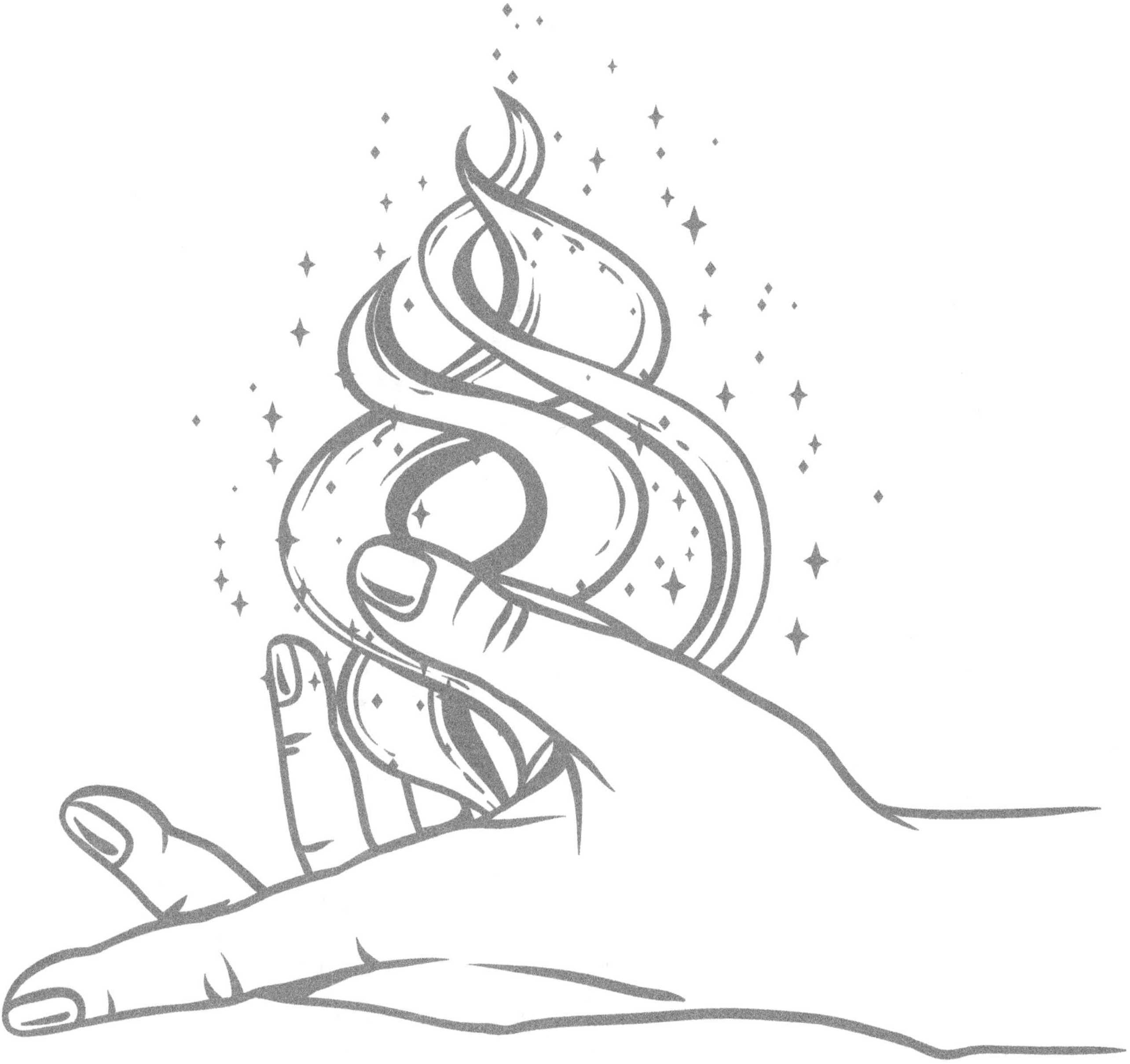

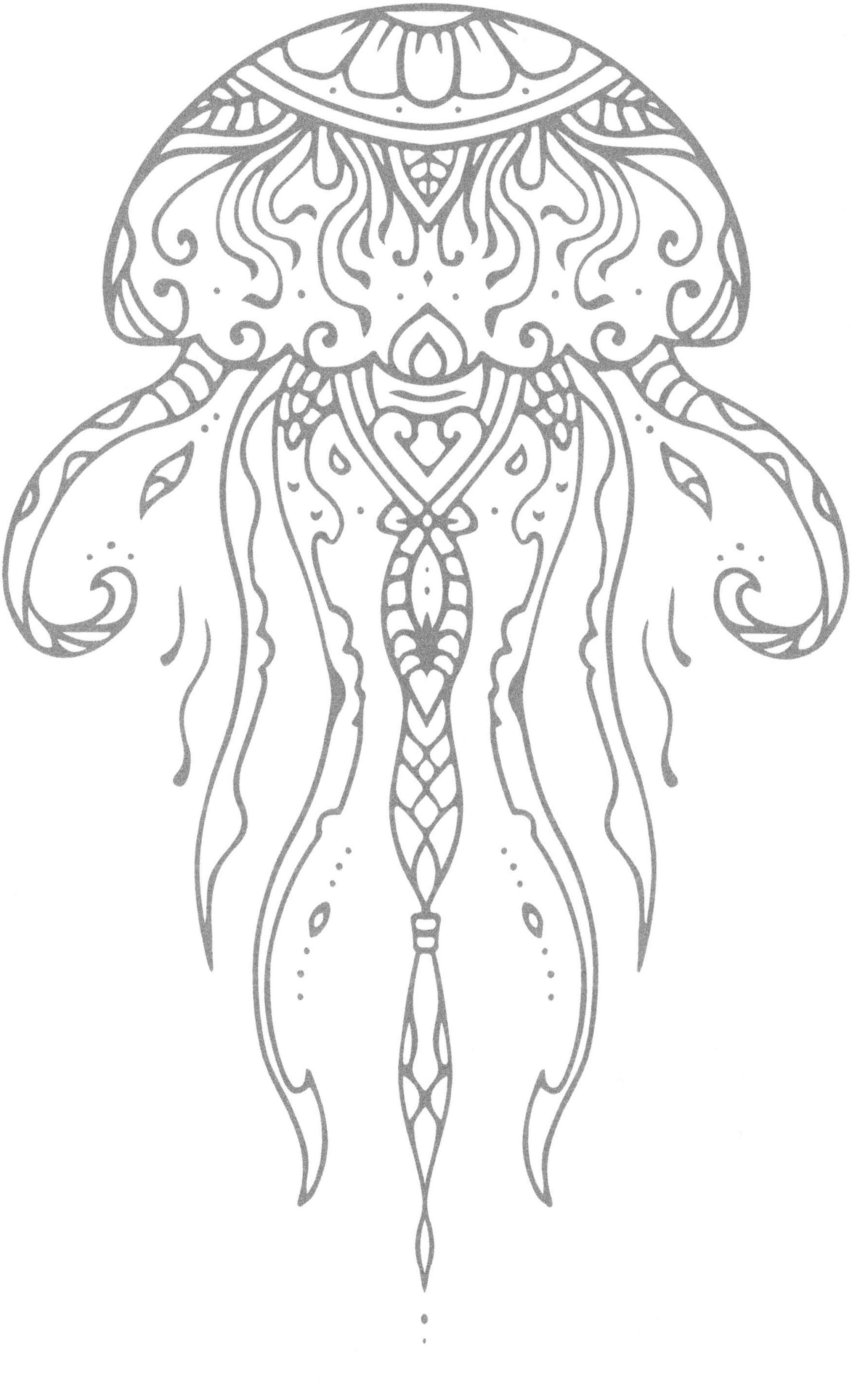

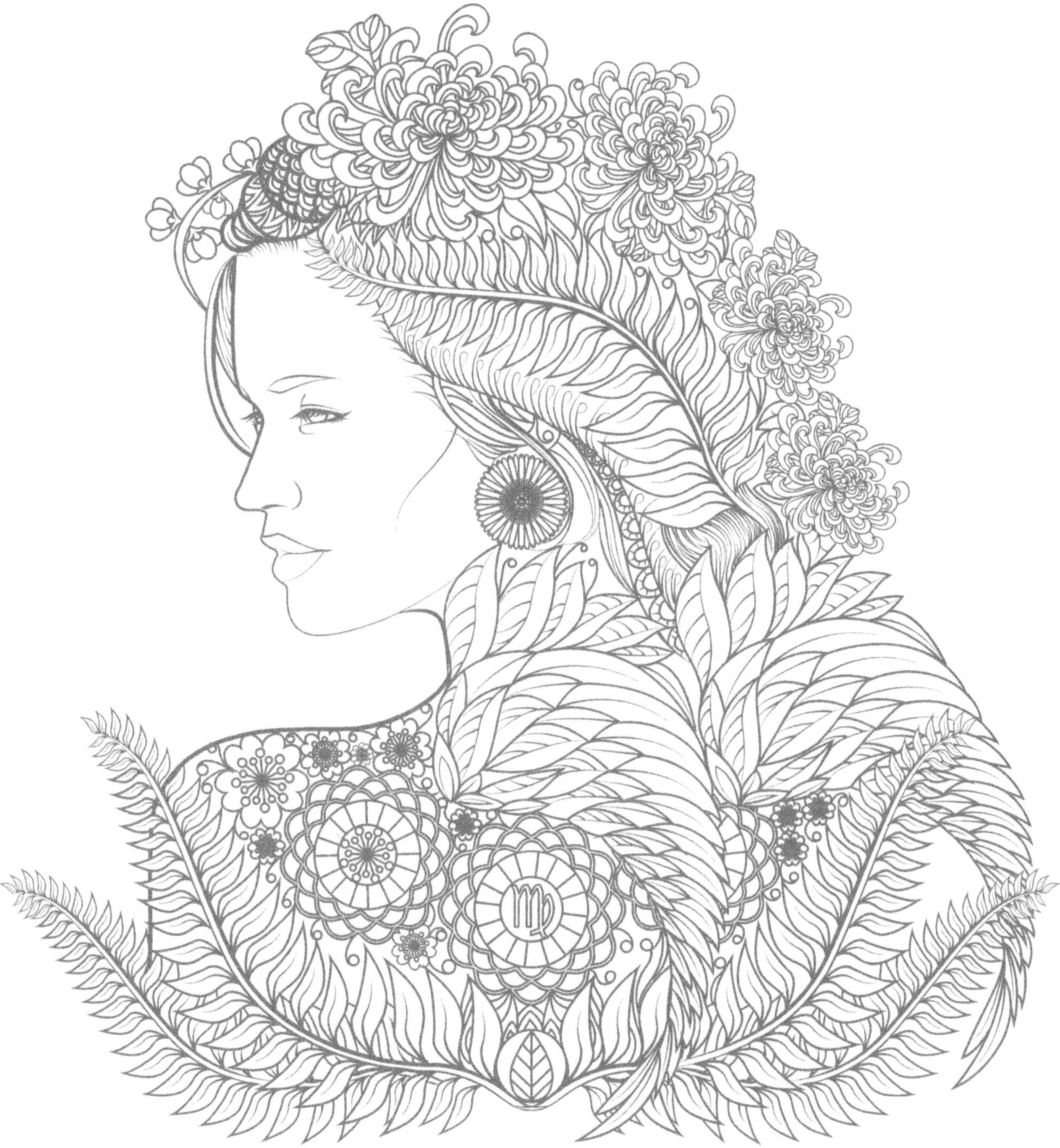

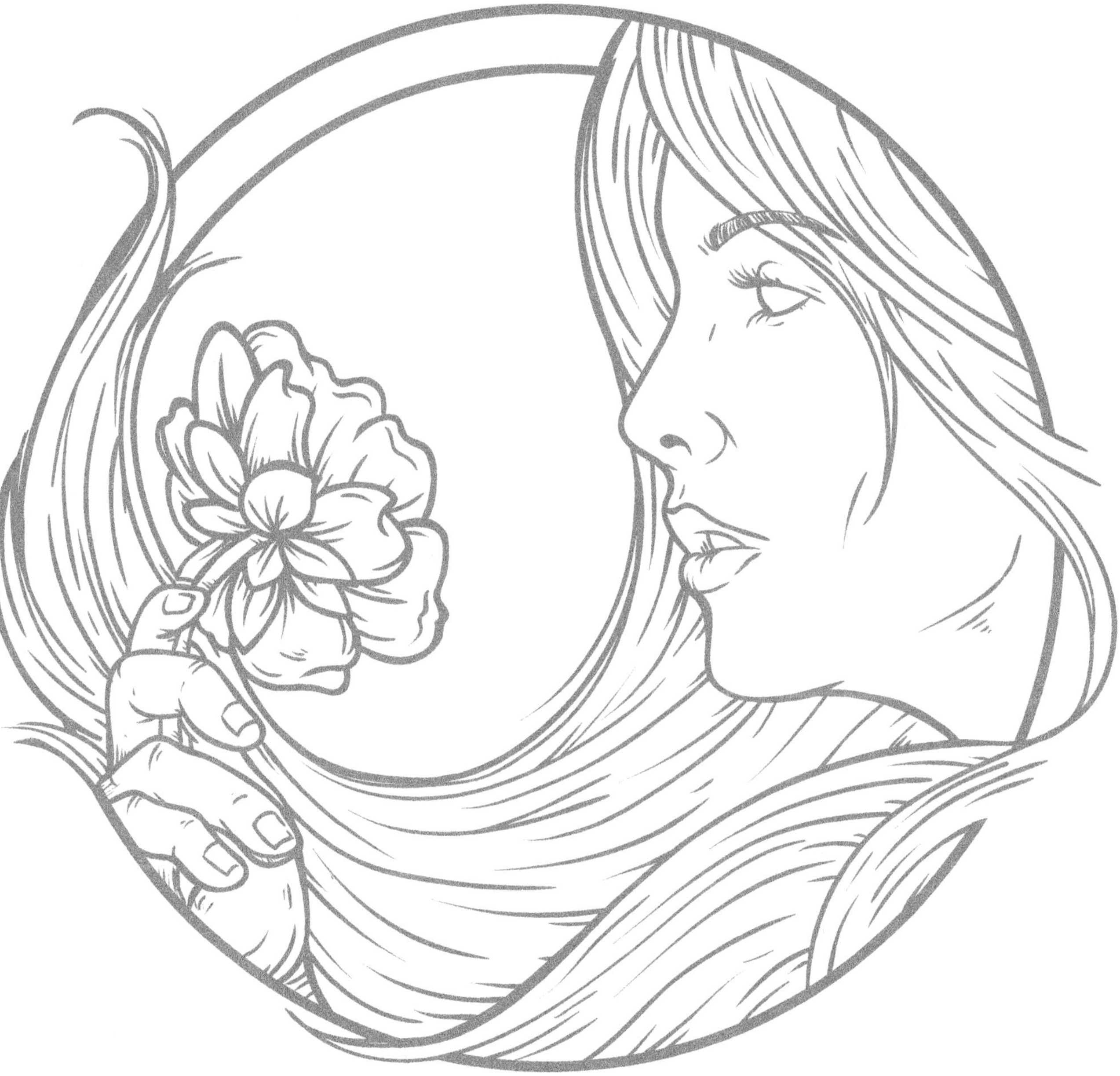

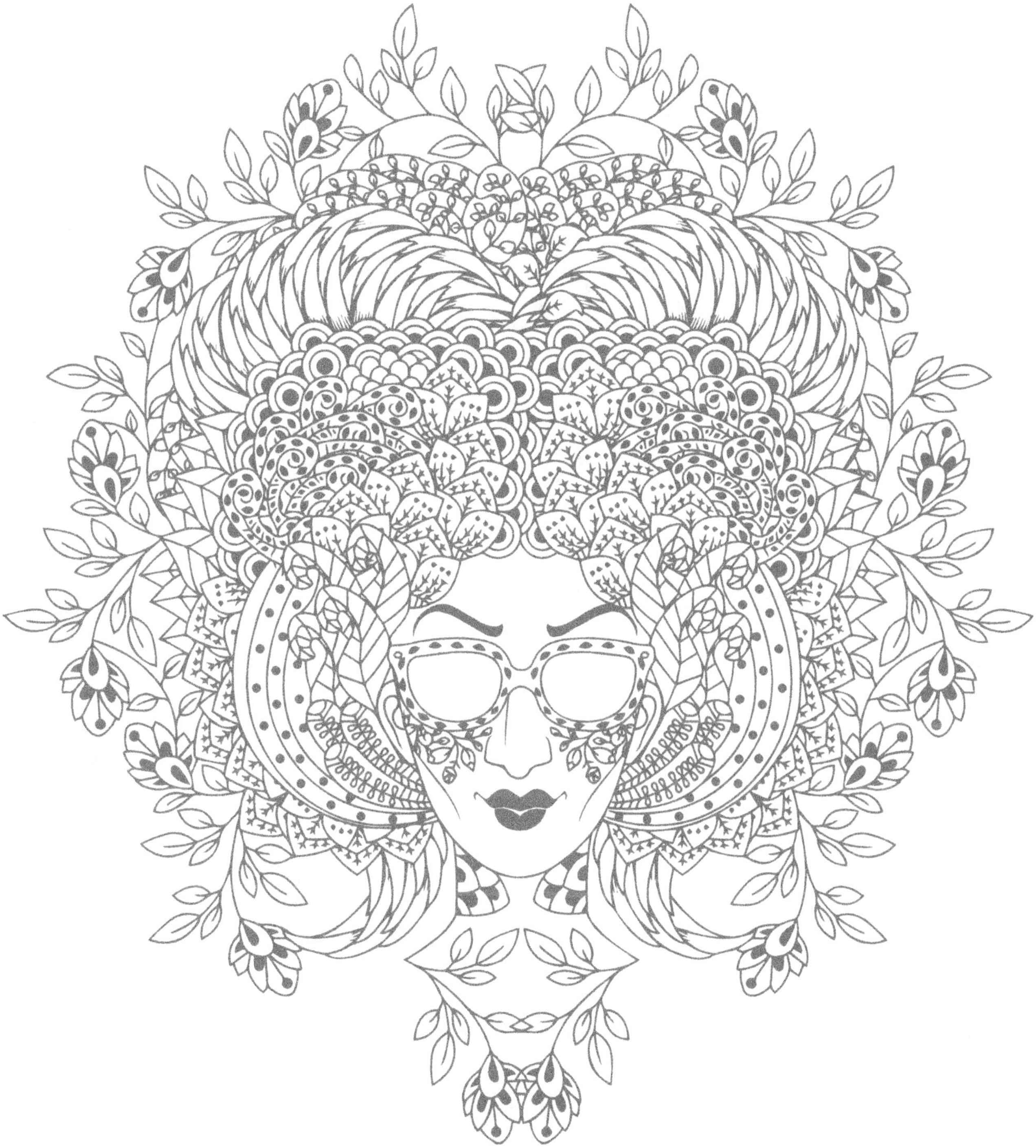

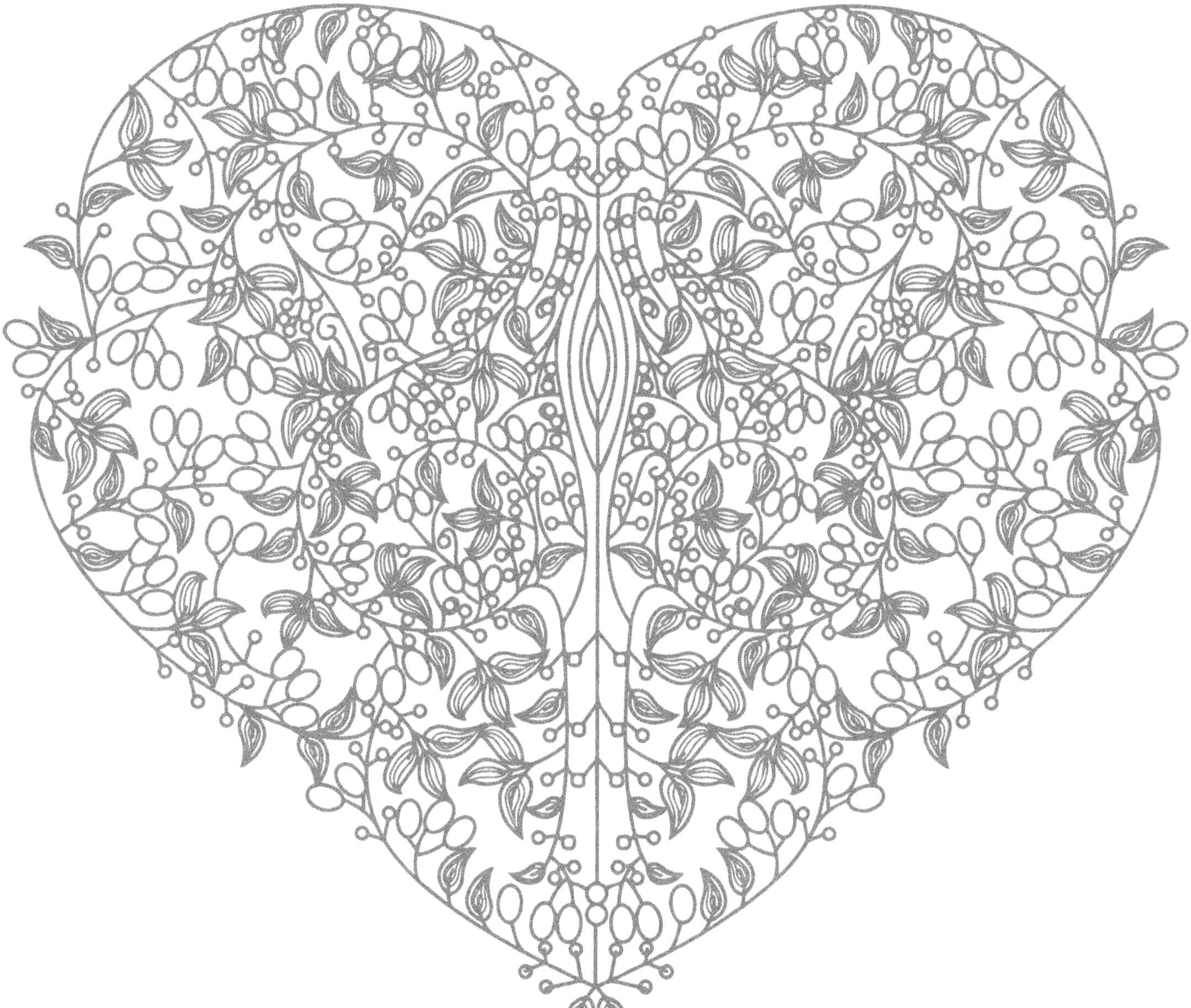

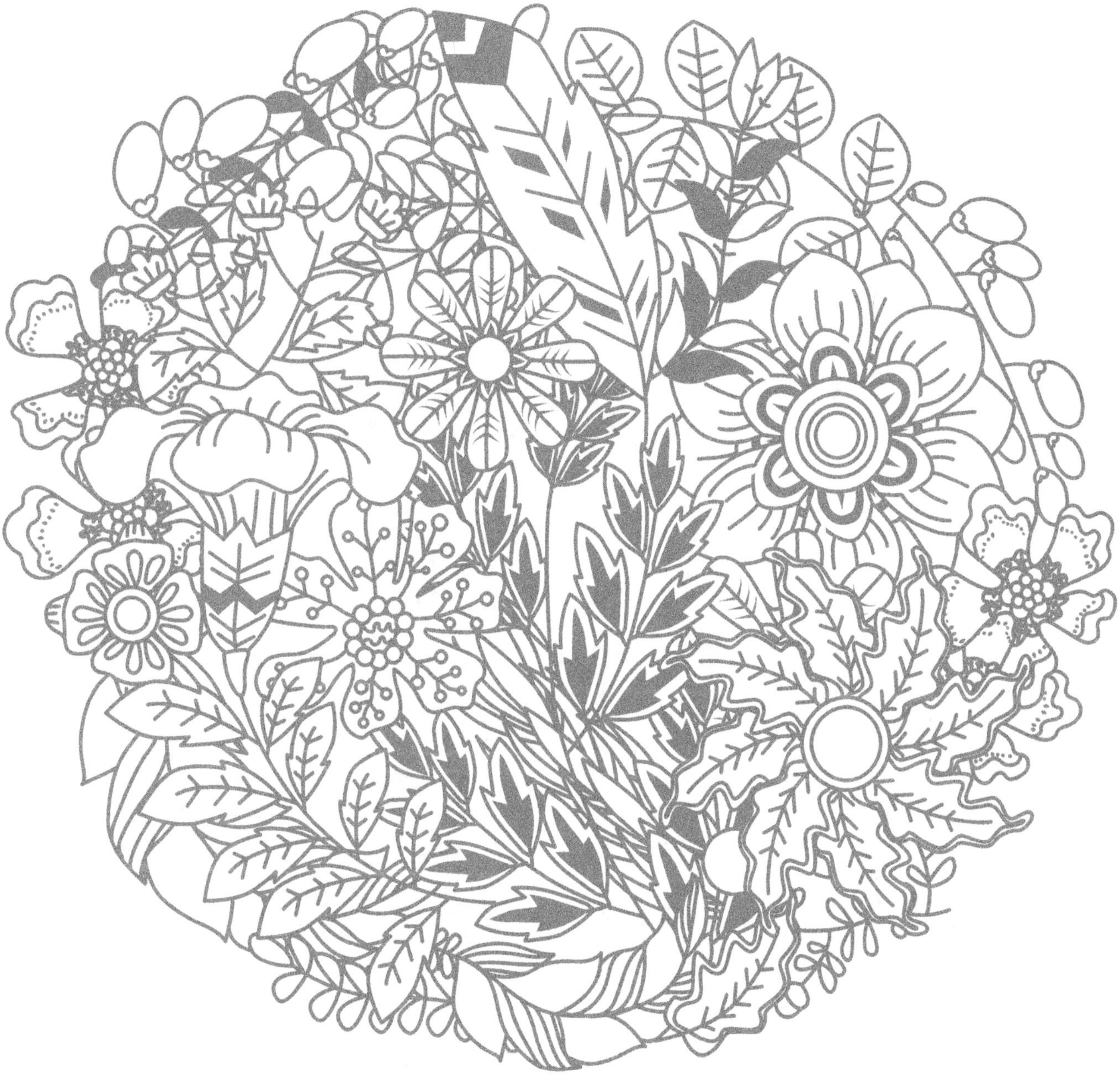

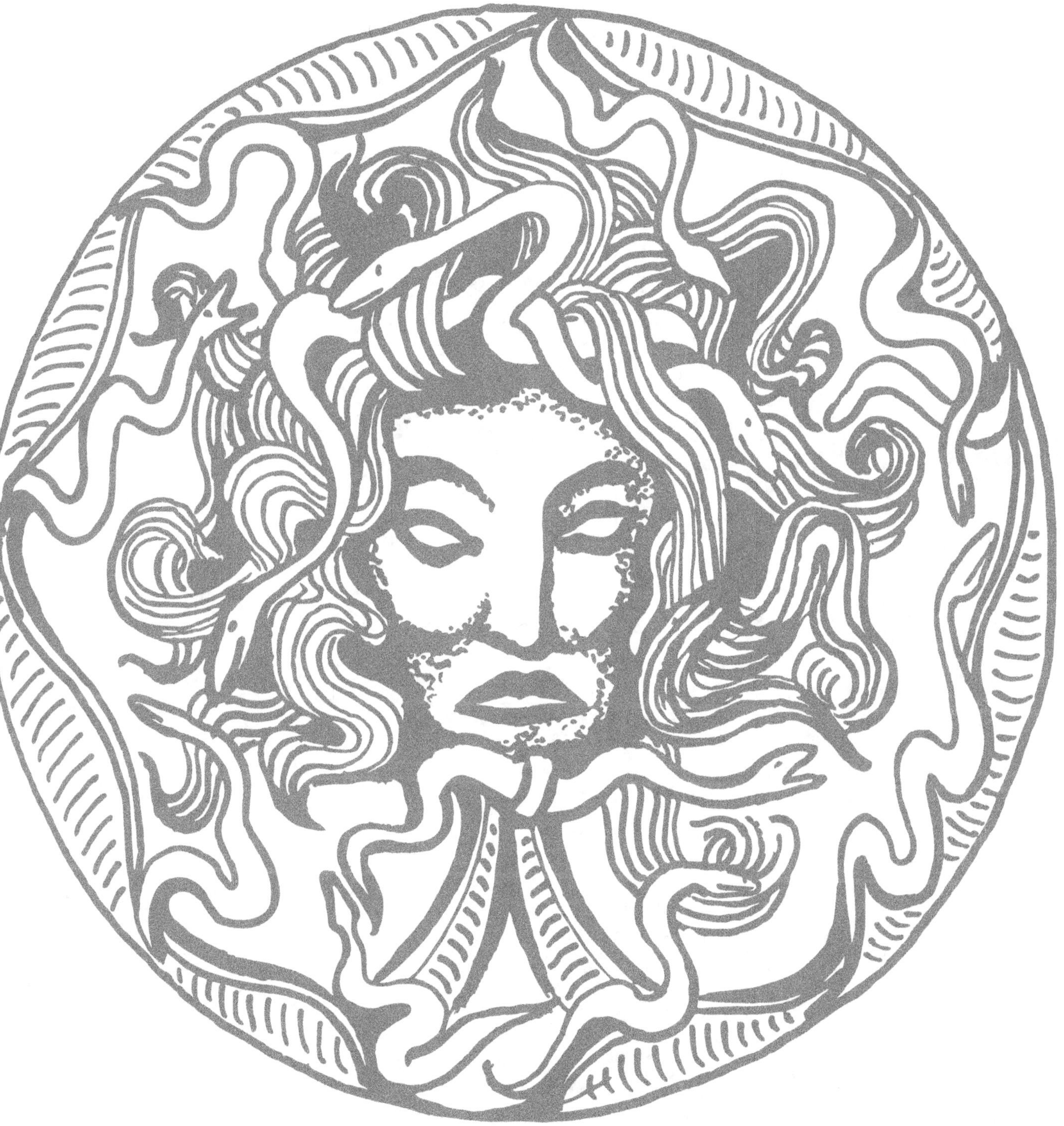

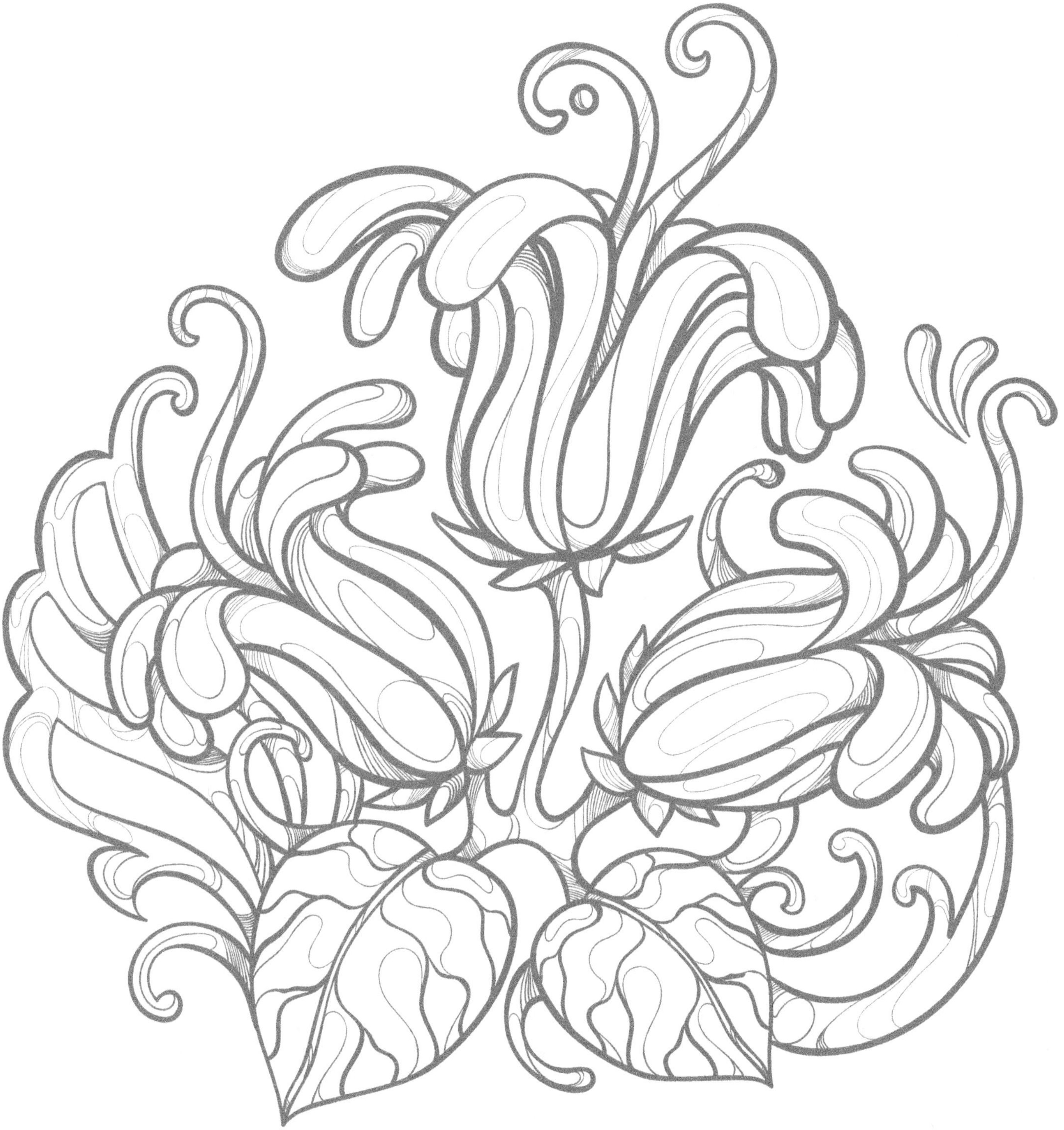

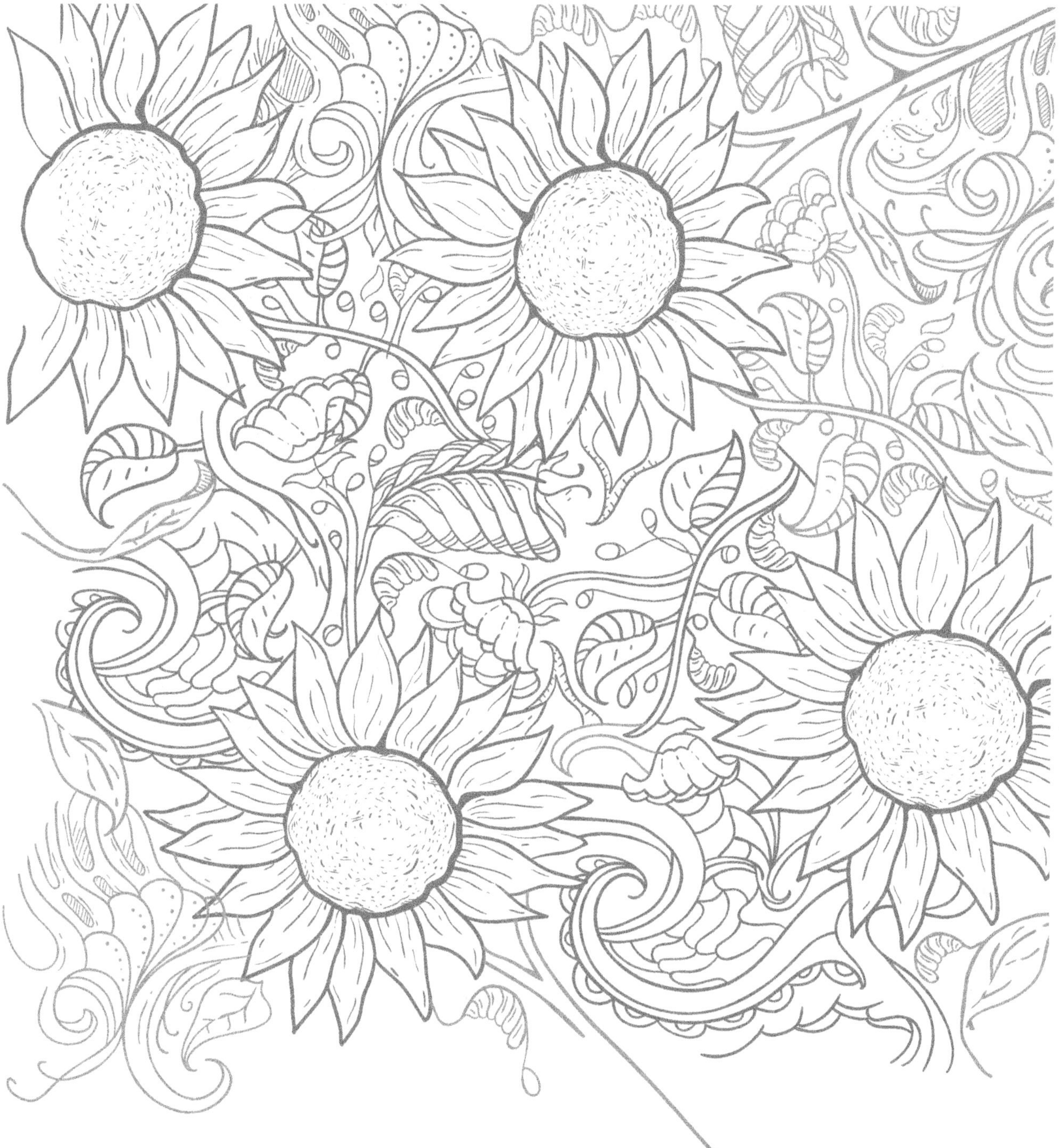

www.ingramcontent.com/pod-product-compliance
Lightning Source LLC
Chambersburg PA
CBHW081447220526
45466CB00008B/2543